Unsung Heroes

Ohioans in the White House:
A Modern Appraisal

Unsung Heroes

Ohioans in the White House:
A Modern Appraisal

By James B. Cash

Orange Frazer Press
Wilmington, Ohio

ISBN: 1-882203-22-4
Copyright 1998 by James Burris Cash

Additional copies of Unsung Heroes or other Orange Frazer Press publications may be ordered directly from:
    Customer Service Department
    Orange Frazer Press, Inc.
    Box 214, 37'/2 West Main Street
    Wilmington, Ohio 45177

Telephone 1.800.852.9332 for price and shipping information

Library of Congress Cataloging-in-Publication Data
Cash, James B. (Burris). 1935-
    Unsung heroes : the Ohio presidents : a modern appraisal / by
James Burris Cash.
        p. cm.
    Includes bibliographic references and index.
    ISBN 1-882203-22-4 (alk. paper)
    1. Presidents--United States--Biography. 2. Ohio--Biography.
I. Title.
E176.1.c263 1998
973'.09'9--dc21   98-23600
                                                      CIP

cover design, Brooke Wenstrup
art direction, John Baskin
photographic manipulation by Tim Thrasher of Thrasher Graphics, Brattleboro, Vermont

Front cover: From left, Rutherford B. Hayes and grandson, Sherman Otis Hayes; William Howard Taft; and Ulysses S. Grant.
Back cover: At bottom left, Benjamin Harrison; at right, James Garfield. Background, from left: William Henry Harrison, William McKinley, and Warren G. Harding with dog, Laddie.

To Nat Lindsey
There could not have been a better friend...

Contents

Introduction

Through our great good fortune in our youth our hearts were touched
by fire.

*—Oliver Wendell Holmes Jr., Civil War veteran and later Supreme Court
Justice, Memorial Day, 1884*

A. What Is This Book About?

This book is about eight individuals chosen for the highest office in
our land. What they did and why they were chosen makes a dramatic story.
It is called *Unsung Heroes.* They are unsung because they don't command
much attention today in our celebrity-obsessed culture. They are called
heroes because all of them took some kind of heroic action during their
lives. I don't want to spoil the plot, but suggest that if you disagree, read
the book, think about our country's principles, and judge for yourself.

The book has eight biographical essays, one for each President, a
concluding chapter entitled *Afterwords,* and an appendix. The appendix is
entitled *Some Comments on Evaluating U. S. Presidents.* Some might characterize
it as a bomb thrown at conventional wisdom. That would be an exaggera-
tion, but I suppose I would say that I find conventional wisdom is too
conventional and not wise enough. You can judge that, too.

There are some other things you should know about the book.

B. Why Eight Presidents?

This book includes essays on eight Ohio Presidents. Most of these
Presidents are clearly Ohioans, but some people might question the inclu-
sion of the two Harrisons, or Grant. William Henry Harrison was born in
Virginia. He left there at age 19 for the Ohio territory. He lived for a
while in Vincennes, Indiana, and other places, including the country of
Colombia, where he tangled with the legendary Simon Bolivar, but his
permanent (non-log cabin) home was in North Bend, Ohio.

His grandson, Benjamin, was born on Harrison land near North Bend.

He grew up there attending school in Cincinnati, and college at Miami in Oxford, Ohio, where he met his wife. He left Ohio at age 20 for Indianapolis. There is a kind of symmetry there: William Henry-Ohio home after age 19; Benjamin-Ohio home first 20 years. I wanted to look at both Harrisons to see what they had in common (courage and dedication, and a remarkable link, John Scott Harrison, son of William Henry and father of Benjamin), and I concluded that they are both important and relevant today, for radically different reasons.

Grant is easier. He was born at Point Pleasant, Ohio and grew up at nearby Georgetown, Ohio. He went off to the military academy, against his will, and had the good and ill fortune of being needed in the army during the Mexican War, and not needed afterwards until the Civil War. He lived at military posts, the home of his wife, Julia, in Missouri, and finally, prior to the Civil War, in Galena, Illinois. From there he re-entered the army. Of all the dramatic lives covered in this book Grant's may have been the most dramatic. I hope my essay communicates that.

The others were unquestionably Ohioans, all their lives. In the nineteenth century, Ohio was a transition state. (My own theory is this is why it and its people achieved so much). Ohio had a large Western Reserve, and most of the Ohio Presidents' families had New England backgrounds. This shows in their culture and basic views.

C. Essays, Not History

I have tried to make these essays as accurate and objective as possible, but the reader should understand that I am a citizen-reader and essayist, not a historian. My goal was to understand the individuals, and what they did, and then put them into the context of their times. The scholar has some advantages. He and she study primary sources. If they are objective and clear, they appropriately lay down the guidelines of what we study as history. A citizen-reader-essayist also has some advantages. For one thing he or she is unlikely to live in an academic world with all its strange biases. Thomas Jefferson observed that the "ploughman's judgment is often better than a professor's, because he has not been led astray by artificial rules." The writer of this book can not claim the distinction of being a ploughman but an operational businessman and former Federal employee of over twenty-five years. My own view is that observant Federal employees who have direct knowledge of government can often understand what works, and what doesn't, and can tell the difference between effective action and rhetoric. They can also be especially sensitive to that bane of modern times, governmental use of public relations.

D. Some Goals of the Book

1. Study Character

Character is important, and I have tried to get at it in a number of different ways. This book differs from many presidential books in that it tries, in a balanced way, to cover the Presidents' entire lives. What they did or did not do as Presidents is consistent with their previously established character. There is a lot in the book about the Civil War because that was a transcendent event for the country and for five of the eight Ohio Presidents.

2. Include the Wives

For every Ohio President, the wife was important. Crete Garfield was her husband's closest advisor. Helen Herron Taft, Julia Grant, and "Duchess" Harding had great ambitions for their husbands. Anna Symmes Harrison and Lucy Webb Hayes were perfect teammates for their husbands. Caroline Scott Harrison created an artistic environment at the White House. One problem with giving appropriate credit to the first ladies is the unavailability of specific information about them. Julia Dent Grant and Helen Herron Taft wrote autobiographies, which were revealing and helpful. There is also a useful biography on the incomparable Lucy Webb Hayes.

3. Let the Presidents Speak for Themselves

You will note that I have included words from the Presidents that are interesting or relevant in each essay. They are revealing because the Ohio Presidents generally wrote their own speeches, which reflect their views and their times. Both Harrisons, Hayes, Garfield, and Taft were highly literate men. U. S. Grant was president of the literary society at West Point. (This may have had much to do with his being a great general). Grant wrote very clearly as a general, and his *Memoirs* is a classic work. Benjamin Harrison's prose descriptions of the Civil War are at times poetic. These words say something about the education of the times, however primitive the facilities. As a kind of amendment to this, I have included words that others have said after the Presidents' deaths. Especially poignant are James G. Blaine's tribute to Garfield, the tribute from an anonymous American Indian for William McKinley, and the belated and sincere eulogy of Warren G. Harding by Herbert Hoover.

4. Include Bibliographies

I probably read 130 books during my writing of this one. I thought most of them were good. Those that I thought were most valuable or useful are included in the general bibliography at the end of the book, or the bibliographies following each presidential essay. You will note there are several novels and plays and histories from other countries. I found these all relevant. It is my hope that this book will lead you to others.

5. Include Pictures to Illustrate Character

A picture is another way of revealing character. For the Ohio Presidents, I found many revealing pictures. One thing to remember is that their contemporaries considered Garfield and McKinley to be handsome men. For the wives, Mrs. Taft's, and Mrs. W. H. Harrison's pictures are perfect. Unfortunately, I haven't found pictures that adequately show Lucy Hayes's graciousness, or Julia Grant's vivacity.

E. A Brief Note on Civil War Terminology

There is a lot in the book about the Civil War. I always call it the Civil War, and never the "War between the States" as some Confederates did. It is tempting to use the term of Hayes and Benjamin Harrison the "War of Rebellion", except at this time, the Civil War is almost a universally accepted term. I try not to use the terms the North and the South because they are inaccurate. Many Kentuckians and Tennesseeans and other southerners fought for the United States against the Confederacy. General

Winfield Scott, the designer of the "Anaconda" strategy, was from Virginia, as was General George Thomas, the "Rock of Chickamauga." Admiral David Farragut was from Tennessee, General Montgomery Meigs, the logistic genius of the War, was born in Georgia. Also "Yanks" and "Yankees" are not appropriate terms for Midwesterners who played a decisive role in the War. Finally, I generally call it the U. S. Army rather than the politically correct term of the time, Union Army, because that is what it was.

F. Errors

To err is human...
    —Latin saying used by Alexander Pope in 1711

There may be some errors in this book. My handwriting (printing really) is difficult to read under the best of circumstances. I used this flawed ability to take complicated notes, make outlines, write essays, and after semi-competently word processing, edit. Most of the essays have been edited more than 40 times. To use a standard government expression, it would not surprise me if, "Errors have been made." If so, they are inadvertent and I'm sorry.

Enjoy.

—James Burris Cash, July, 1998

Hail Columbia! Happy land!
Hail ye heroes! heaven born band!
Who Fought and bled in Freedom's cause
Hail Columbia!

—Joseph Hopkinson

William Henry Harrison
Cincinnatus from Cincinnati

9th President
March 4, 1841–April 4, 1841

At their worst, aristocrats sit around, resting on their ancestors' laurels. They often stop genuine political reform, blocking more talented people. Sometimes aristocrats are inspired to live up to the achievements of their ancestors. William Henry Harrison was one of those. Born a British citizen in Tidewater Virginia, he was the youngest of seven children. He was not in a strong position of inheritance. It was decided early that William Henry would have to be a learner. While at college studying medicine, his father died. William Henry was essentially on his own. He joined the army and went westward to Fort Washington (later a part of Cincinnati). He had some impressive qualities. He was singled out for leadership by Generals Wilkinson, St. Clair, and Wayne. He learned from them all, but especially Wayne. He earned fame in the pre-emptive strategic strike (but surprise counter-attack) against the Shawnee Prophet, Tenskwatawa, Tecumseh's brother. In the almost totally disastrous War of 1812, he defeated a British force and the great Tecumseh himself. Politically, he might have been a mediator between his native South and the free states of the Northwest that he loved. We'll never know.

◄ *General Harrison: The public knew him best as a soldier, not as a politician.*

"The principles upon which our glorious Union was formed, and by which it can be maintained...(are) those feelings of regard and affection...manifested in the first dawn of our Revolution, which induced every American to think that an injury inflicted upon his fellow citizen, however distant his location, was an injury to himself, which made us, in effect, one people..."
—Speech at Cheviot, Ohio, July 4, 1833

●**Family Heritage:** William Henry Harrison was born February 9, 1773, in Charles City County, Virginia, located on the James River, upriver from Williamsburg. William Henry was the youngest of seven children of Elizabeth Bassett and Benjamin Harrison V. The Harrisons became part of the Virginia establishment-American aristocrats. The first Benjamin Harrison emigrated to Virginia from England in 1632. The first five Benjamin Harrisons were political and social leaders in Virginia, and Benjamin Harrison V was a signer of the Declaration of Independence and a friend of George Washington and other colonial leaders. In Benjamin V's last try for political office he was defeated for Congress by John Tyler, whose son would become Vice President for William Henry Harrison. W. H. Harrison was the last United States President born a British subject.

●**Religion:** Harrison was moderately religious, often attending an Episcopalian service Sunday mornings, and a Presbyterian service Sunday evenings.

●**Education:** Harrison studied classical languages, geography, history, mathematics, and rhetoric at Hampden-Sidney College in Virginia. He left to study medicine at College of Physicians and Surgeons, Philadelphia, then left without a degree after his father died, to join the army as an ensign. After moving to what became the Cincinnati area, he studied the Indian mounds of southern Ohio and what became Indiana, and wrote his findings about them. He also collected mastodon teeth. The studies that seemed to interest Harrison most were science, classical studies, rhetoric, and history, especially that of the Roman republic.

●**Wife:** Harrison married Anna Tuthill Symmes, November 25, 1795. Anna was born at Flatbrook near Morristown, New Jersey, July 25, 1775. As a child she was carried through the British lines during the Revolutionary War, by her father, John Cleves Symmes. Symmes was a New Jersey Supreme Court Justice who later became the owner of more than one million acres between the Little Miami and the Great Miami rivers from what became the Cincinnati area to the Dayton—

Springfield area. Her grandparents were from Long Island. Symmes opposed the marriage of his daughter to Harrison, whom he didn't think could make an adequate living. The two married, in defiance of his wishes.

Anna, an independent thinker who exerted a strong influence on her husband, organized their home for almost continuous visitors, many of them distinguished, and conversed with them as an intellectual equal. She also enforced Sabbath rules on her husband. The Harrisons had ten children, two of whom lived beyond the age of 40. Anna lived to be 89. She strongly encouraged her grandson, Benjamin Harrison, to fight for the anti-slavery cause in the Civil War.

The emoluments of my office afford me a decent support and will I hope from henceforth enable me to lay up a small fund for the education of my children. I have hitherto found, however, that my nursery fills up much faster than my strongbox and if our future progress is as great has it has been and our Government should adopt the Roman policy of bestowing rewards on those who contribute most to the population of the Country I do not despair of obtaining the Highest premium.
—Letter to President Jefferson, July 5, 1806

●**Professions:** At age 19, in 1791, Harrison struck out on his own by becoming a junior officer assigned to Fort Washington, (Cincinnati) Ohio. He served under Generals Arthur St. Clair, James Wilkinson, and "Mad" Anthony Wayne. He impressed all three, especially Wayne, who became Harrison's mentor and idol. Harrison was friendly, studious, respectful, deliberate, and energetic. In 1796 Harrison left the army to become secretary to Governor St. Clair, of the Northwest Territories. In 1799 he was elected a delegate to the Sixth Congress. Later he became Governor of the Indiana Territory for eleven years, a general of regular troops and state militias at Tippecanoe and in the War of 1812. He was also an investor, farmer, state senator, U. S. Congressman, Senator, and Minister to Colombia. When he was nominated for President, he was clerk of common pleas for Hamilton County, Ohio.

●**Residences:** Harrison's main residence was North Bend, Ohio, at the north bend of the Ohio River between Cincinnati and the Indiana border. Harrison enlarged his home several times and eventually it had 22 rooms, but the original wing was framed in logs. This was what was later referred to as a "log cabin" in the 1840 campaign. In Indiana, Harrison built a home, "Grouseland," which is still standing in Vincennes, the territorial capital.

(In leading Western troops) the tongue and the pen were as important as the sword.
   —To James Brooks, editor, New York *Express*, 1840

●**Personal Characteristics:** Harrison was slender, of average height, and a sallow complexion. Although he was informal and personable, he communicated great confidence and was popular with Western soldiers, many of whom had short term enlistments in state militias. Harrison also had the respect of professional soldiers. His troops appreciated his imagination, informality, generosity, and courage. He was generally a cautious commander, a quality criticized by some. But he participated in the Fallen Timbers victory as an aide and in two other great victories as a commander. Harrison's hospitality generally exceeded his pocketbook, which sometimes contributed to financial difficulties. His talkativeness got on the nerves of some people, including John Quincy Adams.

The American Backwoodsman—clad in his hunting shirt, the product of his domestic industry, and fighting for the country he loves, he is more than a match for the vile but splendid mercenary of a European monarch.
   —From speech, probably in 1812

~
Part I: Political and Military Career

When Harrison came to Ohio in 1791, it was mostly forested. There were oaks, sycamores, beech, elms, ashes, poplars, and other trees that approached the size of the California redwoods. Game was everywhere, including bison and elk. Fish could be speared in the rivers. The main inhabitants of Ohio, various Indian tribes, were not unified but in general sensed that they were given the land and its resources by the Great Spirit. The Indians called the Ohio, "the beautiful river," and many of the settlers agreed. The settlers, who sought economic freedom, planned to cut down the trees and use the land for farming. One of the purposes of the army was to keep the peace between the settlers and the Indians.

Harrison's initial impression of the army was not good. There was much heavy drinking and the fighting of duels. He stayed away from both, mainly reading and studying. This apparently impressed all his commanders, especially "Mad" Anthony Wayne, who made Harrison an aide. Wayne, a Revolutionary War hero, had been warned by George Washington about Indian tactics: They often

Artist's depiction of a meeting between Tecumseh and General Harrison at Grouseland

stole supplies, and picked the sites of battle to their own advantage. An Indian coalition, led by Little Turtle of the Miami and Blue Jacket of the Shawnee, had badly defeated the disorganized American troops, first under General Josiah Harmar and then General Arthur St. Clair. The cautious Wayne drilled his troops relentlessly and by building and supplying forts from Hamilton to Eaton, and up the western part of what became the state of Ohio, won a great victory over the Indian coalition at Fallen Timbers, near Toledo, August 20, 1794. After their defeat, the Indians were denied entry into Fort Miami by the British (*perfidious Albion**), who had encouraged the Indians to fight but who were not at war with the United States. Wayne commended Harrison for his courage and leadership at Fallen Timbers.

After the death of Wayne, Harrison resigned from the army to farm and become involved in government. He became secretary to Governor St. Clair and, later, a congressional delegate of the Northwest Territory. In Congress, against the wishes of a powerful lobby of land speculators, he jointly introduced a bill for

*Perfidious Albion essentially means "deceitful England." It dates from the 1600s but was made famous by Napolean in the 1800s.

the Federal Government to open land offices in Steubenville, Marietta, Chillicothe, and Cincinnati to sell land in small parcels and on generous terms to settlers with limited resources.

If he is really a prophet, ask of him to cause the sun to stand still, the moon to alter its course, the rivers to cease to flow, or the dead to rise from their graves.
   —Harrison statement to Delaware Indians about the
Shawnee Prophet, Tenskwatawa (estimated 1811)

A. Governor of Indiana Territory—The Battle of Tippecanoe

From 1800-1812 Harrison was governor of the Indiana Territory. As governor of the Indiana Territory he carried out the policies of Jefferson and Madison, trying to turn the Indians into farmers and having them cede much of their land to the United States. In 1811 he led a military force against Prophetstown on the Tippecanoe River in Battleground (near Lafayette), Indiana. Under the leadership of Tecumseh's mystical brother, Tenskwatawa, The Prophet, the Indians attacked out of the dark while the troops were illuminated by their campfires. It was a bloody battle costing Harrison's troops 179 casualties, including two leaders of the Kentucky Militia, Abraham Owen and Joseph Daviess Ultimately, however, Harrison's troops prevailed through discipline and leadership.

Don't give up the ship!
   —The dying words of Capt. James Lawrence, June 1, 1813

We have met the enemy and he is ours.
   —Oliver Hazard Perry to Harrison, September 10, 1813

B. The War Of 1812

Harrison returned to the military in the War of 1812. Following the deliberate military practices of General Wayne, and after having supplies literally bogged in the Great Black Swamp of northwest Ohio, Harrison was criticized for being too slow. Generally the War did not go well in the East, or the Northwest. The grand strategy was to seize Canada. The ancient General William Hull was sent to Detroit with U. S. Army troops but when threatened by troops under British General Issac Brock, gave up without a fight. General James Wilkinson, a Tennes-

Harrison was the last President born as a British subject and in the War of 1812, he defeated British forces.

see politician, was badly defeated at River Raisin, between Detroit and Toledo. Fort Dearborn (Chicago) fell and was burned. Fort Wayne and Fort Harrison in the Indiana Territory were besieged as were Fort Meigs (Maumee) and Fort Stephenson (Fremont). Harrison, who slowly acquired and forwarded supplies toward northern Ohio, relieved Fort Wayne, and defeated the British and Indian forces at Fort Meigs. (The fort was well designed for defense, and a group of Kentucky Militia captured the attacking British artillery). At Fort Harrison and Fort Stephenson, a 28-year-old captain (and later U. S. president) named Zachary Taylor and George Croghan, a 21-year-old major, heroically held their troops together and withstood the sieges.

Supplies were crucial to both sides. While Harrison was building and provisioning forts heading towards Detroit and Canada, Oliver Hazard Perry was building ships at Presque Isle (near Erie, Pennsylvania). When Perry was ready with the ships, he lacked sailors to man them. Many who volunteered were militiamen and free blacks. Harrison also sent volunteers, some of whom were marksmen, who fired at the British sailors. The story is a dramatic one, Perry losing his flagship, *The Lawrence,* abandoning it, rowing to *The Niagara,* and winning final victory.

After Perry's victory on Lake Erie, the British positions were unsupportable. Using Perry's ships, and those captured from the British, Harrison ferried his troops across Lake Erie. The British and their Indian allies ran and Harrison and his troops followed. They caught up to the enemy near a small Moravian village on the Thames River in Ontario. In this battle, the great Shawnee leader Tecumseh died. Thus Harrison, along with Andrew Jackson, Zachary Taylor, Lewis Cass (a former resident of Marietta, Ohio), and Winfield Scott, became one of the great military heroes of the War of 1812—"Old Buckeye," "George Washington of the West," the "Eagle of the West."

The exports of Ohio are generally the substantial comforts of life...Alas!
that there should be an exception, that a soil that is so good, should be a perversion
of the intentions of the Creator, be made to yield that which is evil—to scatter life
and death with equal burden...I speak of converting the staff of life (to) destruction
of health and happiness...
  —1831 speech before the Hamilton County Agriculture Society
      on the evils of liquor

~

Part II: Civil Life, 1813–1840

After the war, Harrison returned to farming, business, and civil government. He served three years in Congress, two years in the Ohio senate, three years in the U. S. Senate, and one year as U. S. Minister to Colombia. There he got embroiled in intrigues involving Simon Bolivar, the great liberator of South America. Through bad luck or poor management, Harrison lost a great deal of money in business. Two of his sons (one an alcoholic) also did, and he assumed their debts. Harrison was always eager to take government jobs, at least partly for the income. When he ran for president, he was clerk of the courts for Hamilton County, Ohio.

Politically Harrison was not strongly partisan. He thought democracy worked when people were considerate of one another, and cared about the fate of the weakest. He idealized the American Revolution and the Roman Republic. He thought there were many parallels between the latter and the United States. His support for individual and states rights put him on both sides of the slavery question. He wanted slavery to end but thought the owners should be compensated. He negotiated and carried out treaties against the Indians, but he did try to control white settlers on Indian lands and prohibit the sale of alcohol to Indians. As a delegate and a Congressman, he supported the sale of low cost land on generous terms. Nationally he opposed Jackson, his fellow general from the War of 1812, whom, he thought, probably abused the powers of the presidency. Like many Westerners, Harrison believed the national government should support internal improvements like roads and canals, and that this policy would help to unify a diverse country. He also believed in a limited presidency. Harrison personally knew the first ten presidents.

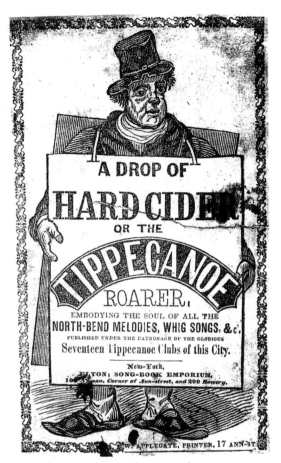

The campaign was modern: personalities not issues.

Part III: Running for President, 1836–1840

A month in the White House: promise unfulfilled

I have never regarded the office of the Chief Magistrate (President) as conferring upon the incumbent the power of mastery over the popular will, but as granting him the power to execute the properly expressed will of the people.

—Speech in 1840

William Henry Harrison ran for President two times. In 1836 the opponents of former president Jackson and the Democratic candidate Van Buren were unable to agree on one candidate, and they thought that possibly by having several, the election would be thrown into the House of Representatives. Harrison was one of the three Whigs to run, coming in second in both popular vote and electoral votes. However Van Buren had a majority of electoral votes and was elected President.

In 1840 the Whigs remained divided on issues. Harrison was picked because of his geniality, the fact that he was not identified with any strong political issues, his family ties to Virginia, Ohio, and Indiana, and his life as a farmer and a soldier, a modern Cincinnatus. In a fateful decision, his running mate, John Tyler, was chosen to win the southern vote.

The 1840 election was non-substantive. This was necessary from the Whig standpoint because any strong commitment on issues would have offended one of their factions and split their coalition. Ironically, the big issue was the "log cabin, hard cider" candidate, Harrison, versus the "silk stocking" candidate, Van Buren. This is one of the first cases of symbolism triumphing over reality. Harrison was born on a large estate of a well-to do Virginia family; his opponent, Van

Buren, was the son of a New York tavern keeper. The campaign was full of rallies, posters, and songs and classified as the first modern campaign. This resulted in the highest percentage vote to that time. Ultimately Van Buren lost, partly because of the campaign but mainly because of the depression of 1837.

~

Part IV: Presidency
March 4–April 4, 1841

A person elected to the (presidency), having his constituents in every section, state and subdivision of the Union, must consider himself bound by the most solemn sanctions to guard, protect and defend the rights of all and of every portion great or small from the injustice and oppression of the rest.
         —Inaugural speech, March 4, 1841

As President, Harrison had limited impact. He appointed a cabinet of unusual talent and merit: Daniel Webster as Secretary of State (Henry Clay refused the post); Thomas Ewing of Lancaster, Ohio, as Secretary of Treasury; John Bell of Tennessee as Secretary of War; John Crittenden of Kentucky as Attorney General, and Francis Granger of New York as Postmaster General. His Cabinet appointees are likely to have been important because Harrison would most likely have listened to and conferred with all of them.

Harrison is famous for having made the longest inaugural address in history, one hour and forty minutes. Ideas excited Harrison and the speech was one of ideas. Undoubtably the speech is easier to read than to listen to, showing a thoughtful and compassionate President. Its first major subject is that of power. It cites the experience of the Romans and the British, and the words of Thomas Jefferson. Harrison pledged to serve only one term, and to use the veto "only to protect the rights and interests of the minority." In the speech, Harrison expressed concern about "metallic money," *i. e.,* gold, and its impact on the weakest. It favored full citizenship for the citizens of the District of Columbia and was skeptical of the role of the political parties.

It said nothing about slavery but, reflecting his own views, Harrison thought the citizens of one state should not interfere with the rights of those in another. He was hopeful that slavery would gradually be abolished without a Civil War. Finally he made a statement in regard to American Indians:

I can conceive of no more sublime spectacle, none more likely to propitiate an impartial and common creator, than a rigid adherence to the principles of justice on the part of a powerful nation in its transactions with a weaker and uncivilized people whom circumstances have placed at its disposal.
—Inaugural Address, March 4, 1841

●Deaths

Sir, I wish you to understand the principles of Government—I wish them carried out—I ask nothing more.
—Last words of William Henry Harrison, April 4, 1841

At age 68 William Henry Harrison was the oldest man elected President. He held that superlative until Ronald Reagan's election in 1980. The election campaign had been grueling, and after his election he was harassed by people seeking favors or jobs. Because of his affable style he was probably overwhelmed, worn down by parties, dinners or receptions. On March 28 he caught a cold, which soon turned into pneumonia. Unfortunately he had the "best medical care" of the day, therefore, he was bled, cupped, doped, and blistered. Death probably seemed easier than continued treatment and on April 4, 1841, he died at the White House. He had served as President for 31 days. He was the first President to die in office.

What soared the old eagle to die at the sun!
Lies he stiff with spread wings at the goal he had won!
Death, Death in the White House! Ah never before
Trod on his skeleton feet on the President's floor!
For the stars on our banner grown suddenly dim,
Let us weep in our darkness, but weep not for him!
Not for him—who in departing leaves millions in tears!
Not for him—who has died full of honor and years!
Not for him who ascended Fame's ladder so high
From the round at the top he has stepped to the sky!
—Last stanza of a widely published poem by Nathaniel P. Willis, April 1841

The North Bend home burned down in 1855. Anna Symmes Harrison died February 25, 1864, at age 88. The Harrisons are buried in a monument overlooking the Ohio River in North Bend.

●Visiting Harrison Sites

Fort Washington no longer exists but was located at approximately Third and Broadway in Cincinnati, near where the Taft Museum is now. There is a marker in downtown Hamiliton where Fort Hamilton once stood. Near Eaton is Fort St. Clair Park, where the Miami Indians defeated a Kentucky Militia. Fort Jefferson State Memorial is near Fort Jefferson south of Greenville off SR 121. The site of Fort Greenville, where the treaty was signed, ceding most of Ohio and parts of Indiana to the U. S. Government, is in downtown Greenville in front of the city building. Fort Recovery, the site of St. Clair's disastrous defeat, is about 37 miles northwest of Greenville. It contains two blockhouses, a stockade wall, and a museum. Defiance includes the sites of Fort Defiance, built by General Wayne, and Fort Winchester, built by General Harrison. The Fallen Timbers Monument (in the wrong place) and Fort Meigs, where the British locked out their Indian allies after their defeat at Fallen Timbers, are in Maumee and Perrysburg near Toledo. Fort Meigs has been reconstructed, and is well worth seeing. The site of old Fort Industry is in Toledo near the present Summit and Monroe Streets. Fort Stephenson no longer exists. Its site is near the public library in Fremont. The Great Black Swamp has been mostly drained, but remnants still exist in the rich farmland of Fulton County near Archbold, Ohio. Perry's victory is commemorated by a memorial at Put-in-Bay, on Lake Erie.

Harrison's ancestral home, "Berkeley," on the James River in Virginia, is open for visitors. The Harrison Mansion in Vincennes, Indiana—"Grouseland"—resembles Berkeley. It is also open to the public.

The site of the Harrisons' home and monument in North Bend can be reached by taking U.S. 50 (River Road) west out of Cincinnati. The Harrisons' monument commands a beautiful view of the Ohio River and an ugly railroad.

●Books Relevant to Understanding the William Henry Harrisons

A. Biographical

Books on William Henry Harrison are somewhat elusive. There are not a lot of books written in the twentieth century about him. Three that come up are:

➡Cleaves, Freeman. 1939. *Old Tippecanoe: William Henry Harrison and His Time.* New York: Scribner's Sons.

This seems to be the most complete, objective, and up-to-date book on Harrison.

➡Goebel, Dorothy Burne. 1926. *William Henry Harrison: a Political Biography.* Indianapolis: Indiana Library and Historical Department.

This book is somewhat dated in its language but otherwise readable. The book she co-wrote that is also cited, *Generals in the White House,* is a very thoughtful and concise work.

➡Green, James A. 1941. *William Henry Harrison: His life and Times.* Richmond, VA: Garrett and Massie, Incorporated.

This is a rather worshipful book about Harrison. It is chatty with many interesting details. It is well-illustrated and has a thorough bibliographic appendix. The author seems to have read everything about Harrison, visited all of the sites (except Colombia), and contacted all of Harrison's descendants.

B. Non-Biographical

I. Roman History

Harrison was impressed by the discipline, simplicity, and zeal of the Roman Republic. The most comprehensive contemporary historian of the Roman Republic is Livy (Titus Livius). Livy wrote in a dramatic and interesting way. He thought we should study history and learn from its examples, good and bad. Three volumes of Livy's history available in Penguin Classic editions are: *The Early History of Rome; The War with Hannibal;* and *Rome and the Mediterranean.* A more recent history of Rome, covering a longer period, is by Will Durant. 1944. *The Story of Civilization,* Volume III, *Caesar and Christ.* New York: Simon and Schuster.

2. War of 1812

●**Horsman, Reginald.** 1969. *The War of 1812*. New York: Arnold A. Knopf.
The War of 1812 is not well understood. The United States was unprepared and the war was a near-disaster. This is an objective account that covers it well, written by a former British citizen who emigrated to America. He explains the positions of both sides.

3. Tecumseh

●**Eckert, Allan W.** 1992. *A Sorrow in Our Heart*. New York: Bantam Books.
Eckert is a prolific writer of Midwest frontier history. Like most of his work this is dramatic and populated with many interesting characters. By reading it one can understand why Tecumseh (born near Xenia, Ohio) remains a legend to this day.

●**Thom, James Alexander.** 1989. *Panther in the Sky*. New York: Ballantine Books.
This provides a different slant on Harrison. This is a good novel sympathetic to Tecumseh, the Shawnees, and his followers from other nations.

●**Tucker, Glenn.** 1956. *Visions of Glory*. Indianapolis: Bobbs-Merrill.
This is a well-written and dramatic biography of Tecumseh.

4. Harrison Home

●**Coski, John M.** 1989. *The Army of the Potomac at Berkeley Plantation; The Harrison's Landing Occupation of 1862*. (This book is available at Berkeley Plantation, 12602 Harrison's Landing Road, Charles City County, VA 23030)
During the Civil War Harrison's birthplace home, strategically located on the James River, became a base of operations for General McClellan's Peninsula campaign. Lincoln met with McClellan and General Daniel Butterfield, and Private Oliver Norton composed "Taps" there. The estate was later purchased by a Union Soldier from Scotland, whose descendants live there today. The book tells the story of McClellan occupation in 1862.

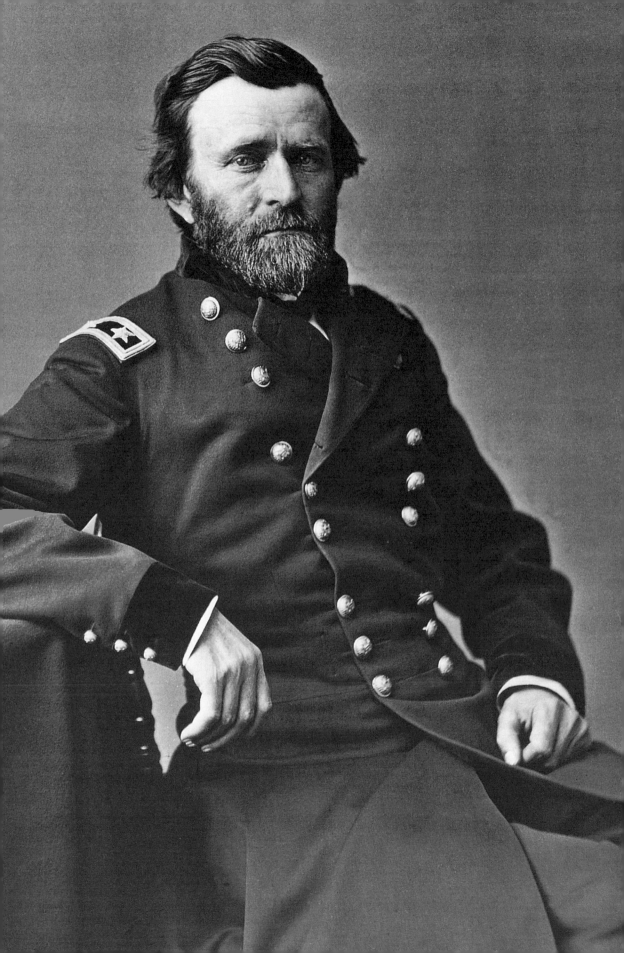

Ulysses S. Grant
Improbable Hero

18th President
March 4, 1869-March 4, 1877

U. S. Grant's life was a strange mixture of glory and failure. Some people never accepted him for what he was. He wasn't tall, he wasn't neat, he wasn't impressive in any conventional way. Befitting his own lack of pretense, he wore a private's uniform in the Civil War. Only the stars on his coat distinguished him. He earned those stars. He organized the strategy that won the Civil War. And afterwards he became President. It was perhaps, after the Civil War, the most difficult time in our history, for us, and him. The rest of his life was more glory, more failure. It culminated in a tragedy worthy of Shakespeare.

I came near forgetting to tell you about our demerit or "black marks" They give a man one of these "black marks" for almost nothing and if he gets 200 a year they dismiss him. To show how easy one can get these a man by the name of Grant...got eight *of these marks fer not going to Church...he was put under arrest so he cannot leave his room perhaps fer a month...We are obliged not only to go to church but must* march *there by companys. This is not exactly republican.*
    —Letter to cousin, R. McKinistry Griffith from West Point, September 22, 1839

◀ *Before the Vicksburg campaign, Mathew Brady photographed Grant in his new uniform.*

One of my superstitions had always been when I started to go any where, or to do anything, not to turn back, or stop until the thing intended was accomplished.
—Memoirs, 1885

●**Family Heritage:** U. S. Grant was born April 27,1822, in Point Pleasant, Ohio, the oldest of six children of Jesse Root Grant and Hannah Simpson Grant. Grant is a Scottish name but his first known American ancestor, Matthew Grant, emigrated from Plymouth, England, to Dorchester, Massachusetts in 1630, and later to Windsor, Connecticut. Ulysses' grandfather, Captain Noah Grant, moved from Windsor to Westmoreland County, Pennsylvania, and eventually Deerfield, Ohio (in 1799). Grant's father, Jesse, entered the tannery business as an apprentice in Maysville, Kentucky. Later he moved to Point Pleasant and then Georgetown, Ohio. He was quite successful, later owning tanneries or stores in Ohio, Kentucky, Illinois, and Wisconsin. He was aggressive and opinionated, causing his son difficulties during the Civil War and later. The family of Hannah Simpson Grant moved from Pennsylvania, to southern Ohio in 1817. Grant's mother was gentle and quiet. Grant's original name was Hiram Ulysses, presumably based upon the Phoenician leader Hiram, and Ulysses of *The Odyssey.*

●**Religion:** Grant was raised a Methodist but was never baptized and had little involvement with any church. He came to believe that the Civil War was punishment for slavery and the Mexican War.

●**Education:** Grant attended private or subscription schools in Georgetown and Ripley, Ohio, and Maysville, Kentucky. At age 17, to his surprise, his father's influence got him appointed by a Congressman to the U.S. Military Academy, replacing an area dropout. The Congressman appointed Grant as "Ulysses Simpson" Grant. Later, Grant, who was self-conscious about the initials "HUG," would change his name to Ulysses S. Grant. His classmates nicknamed him "Uncle Sam," and thereafter he was to many of them, Sam. Grant enjoyed the camaraderie of West Point and was admired by many of his peers. He was good in mathematics, outstanding in horsemanship, and had some skill in drawing. He also enjoyed literature and became president of the literary society, and he liked to travel. Grant was not a neat dresser and did not do well under military discipline, earning many demerits. When he left West Point he was assigned to the infantry, rather than the cavalry, his first choice, or engineering, the choice of most of the top students.

I don't feel like fighting, Jess, but I can't stand being hectored by a man of your size.
—U. S. Grant to his two-year-old son in 1860

●**Wife:** When Grant visited the family of his roommate, Frederick S. Dent, in the St. Louis area, he fell in love with Dent's sister, Julia. Grant was short, shy, and modest but always somewhat handsome. Julia was outgoing and friendly but had an eye defect that made her somewhat self-conscious. They shared a love of literature. Her father, a slave owner, was not impressed with Grant's prospects. Ulysses and Julia endured a four-year engagement, mostly while he was off fighting in the Mexican War. They were married in St. Louis, August 22, 1848. James Longstreet, a friend of Grant and later a Confederate general, was a groomsman for

"The boy is too poor," Julia's father said of Grant.

Grant. Julia probably always recognized Grant's innate talents and natural generosity and was always ambitious for him. Moreover she loved the limelight and the life of Washington and New York. He was indifferent to ambition but tolerant of Julia's goals. He just always sought to do his job. The Grants had three sons and a daughter, all of whom lived into the twentieth century.

Gen. Grant is my admirable Crichton. He is brave, he is kind, he is just, he is true.
—Julia Dent Grant to W. T. Sherman

●**Personal Characteristics:** Grant was a short, quiet, informal, and unassuming man with an ironic sense of humor. He was a listener, a careful observer, and a life-long learner. As a general, he took a fundamental approach, always keeping the big picture in mind and understanding how every battle fit in to it. When he could, he positively reinforced his officers and men with praise. He had a great talent for seeing things objectively and adjusting to a new reality. He blamed the generals at Shiloh and the Wilderness, including himself, and not the troops. He was also sensitive and generous. At Appomattox, he stopped the celebrations by his own troops at the surrender of "our own countrymen."

Part I: The Civil War
Grant Achieves Greatness
in the West, 1861-1864

Noteriety has no charms for me and could I render the same services that I hope has been my fortune to render our just cause, without being known in the matter, it would be infinately prefferable (sic) to me.
—Letter, U. S. Grant to Congressman Elihu B. Washburne, May 14, 1862

You have no conception of the amount of labor I have to perform. An army of men all helpless looking to the commanding officer for every supply. Your plain brother however has, as yet, had no reason to feel himself unequal to the task and fully believes he will carry on a successful

Young Grant, age 21, fresh from West Point.

campaign against our rebel enemy. I do not speak boastfully but utter a presentiment. The scare and fright of the rebels up here is beyond conception. Twenty three miles above here (in Tennessee) some were drowned in their haste to retreat thinking us such Vandals that neither life nor property would be respected...
—Letter to Mary Grant (sister) February 9, 1862

Don't be too anxious about what the other fellow is going to do to you, but make him anxious about what you are going to do to him.
—Memoirs, 1885 (This quote shows that Grant's objectivity and insight was based upon his early experience in Missouri and Tennessee. With this view, it is not surprising that Grant became an offensive general.)

Grant's story is that of the unplanned life; or classical tragedy; or fate. As a quiet man he was almost always underestimated. He had modest ambitions, desiring to be a farmer in southern Ohio, or a math teacher. He was kind and generous, willing to work hard. It is likely his hard-driving, opinionated father saw something lacking in young Ulysses and thus had him appointed to West Point. Young Ulysses didn't want to go to West Point (other than for the travel and the opportunity it gave him to see new places). He didn't like the military discipline nor did he want to be in the army. When it came time to serve his army obligation he was sent to the infantry, despite his acknowledged skill in horsemanship. And in the infantry he became a quartermaster, or commissary officer, not a leader of troops. Like many things, he accepted this with quiet determination. He fought in the Mexican War with courage and common sense, receiving some recognition as a supply officer and a fighter, even though he (like Thoreau) did not think the war was just.

After the war, he traveled around Mexico to satisfy his curiosity. His post war assignments were mostly boring and meaningless. And he tolerated the inanities of military discipline. After he left the army in 1854 he failed as a farmer, a real estate worker, and began cutting wood and selling it in St. Louis. After the panic of 1857, he pawned his watch to buy Christmas gifts for his family. On the streets of St. Louis he met another West Pointer whose name would be linked inextricably with his: William Tecumseh Sherman, also down on his luck. They looked like a couple of bums. This was the context, at age 38, in which he asked his father for a job, and it took him to Galena, Illinois.

The 1860 election of Abraham Lincoln caused South Carolina to secede. Eventually, ten other states joined South Carolina in the Confederate States of America (CSA). In April of 1861, the Confederates attacked a United States fort in the Charleston (South Carolina) harbor, and the Civil War began. The United States put out a call for volunteers and Grant, who believed in his country and was mildly anti-slavery, offered to help. The initial call-ups were heavily oversubscribed and somewhat chaotic. The calm Grant brought organization, skill, and discipline to the task. He did so well at the local level (Galena, Illinois) that he was called to the state level. There, he was kept on for weeks. He retained a modest view of his own skills and applying to become a colonel in the U.S. Army, he thought himself somewhat unequal to the task. After observing many of the colonels from Illinois and Indiana, however, he understood he could do as well. Later, he would go to see Major General George McClellan, an impressive general in every way except the ability to pursue the enemy and to win battles. Grant was unable to get a meeting with McClellan. In the meantime, Grant became a colonel, and then a brigadier general in the Illinois Militia.

When the militia was federalized, Grant became a colonel in the U.S. Army. He started by having his troops guard railroad lines and trestles in Missouri. An early strategic prize of the war was Kentucky, which had declared its neutrality. General Gideon Pillow, CSA, made a strategic blunder by occupying Columbus, Kentucky, and thereby offending many Kentuckians. Making his headquarters at Cairo, Illinois, at the junction of the Ohio and Mississippi rivers, Grant then occupied Paducah and Smithland, important river junctions in Kentucky. In 1862 he proposed to attack Forts Donelson and Henry on the Cumberland and Tennessee rivers in Tennessee. Permission was reluctantly given by Major General Henry W. Halleck (Old Brains), an ambitious intellectual general and astute bureaucrat who eventually became chief of staff in Washington.

Working with Flag Officer Foote of the U. S. Navy, Grant conquered both forts. When asked for terms, he specified at Fort Donelson "...unconditional and immediate surrender." This was the first major victory by the U. S. Army in the Civil War, and the newspapers restated his name as "Unconditional Surrender" Grant. A gratified Lincoln promoted Grant to major general.

Grant got in trouble at least three times with General Halleck. Grant had tried to stop trade with the confederates and investigated crooked supply contractors. He made enemies and rumors of his drinking on duty began. An inter-

July 3, 1863: Grant received message from Confederate General Pemberton asking about surrender of Vicksburg.

esting story related to that situation is that of then Major James B. McPherson ("beloved McPherson" of Clyde, Ohio). McPherson, an engaging and personable officer, was one of the bright young men of the U.S. Army, first in the West Point class of 1854. He was an engineering officer on Halleck's staff. Halleck transferred him to Grant's staff with the condition that McPherson find out about Grant's drinking. It is not known how McPherson handled the assignment, but he soon became one of Grant's key subordinates and good friends.

McClellan, another engineering officer and then general-in-chief, probably never liked Grant because of Grant's unmilitary style. There was also a period where Halleck said he never heard from Grant. Finally, the battle of Shiloh, a close and costly victory, led Halleck to take over the field command of Grant's army and to give Grant a meaningless assignment. Grant asked to resign but key people intervened: General William Tecumseh Sherman; Senator John Sherman (of Lancaster and Mansfield, Ohio), and William's brother; and Grant's Congressman, Elihu Washburne. It is never clear if Halleck supported Grant or not, but he refused to accept Grant's resignation. Lincoln had never met Grant, but liked him as a general "who fights."

Grant was restored to his command and went on to victories in Tennessee and Mississippi. This culminated in a great victory after a siege at Vicksburg, Mississippi, "the Gibraltar of the South," on July 4, 1863, which opened the entire Mississippi River to the United States forces. With the great defensive victory under General Meade at Gettysburg, Pennsylvania, on the same day, it became for the United States the greatest day of the Civil War.

After the conquest of Vicksburg, Grant appointed General McPherson military governor. He showed great resourcefulness and compassion to the citizens of Vicksburg and was criticized by some Unionist papers. Grant supported him as implementing a policy to win back the loyalty of the citizens of Vicksburg.

When General Rosecrans and the Army of the Cumberland lost at Chickamauga (in a battle involving future President, James A. Garfield), and backed away to Chattanooga, the western armies were consolidated under Grant. He promoted Generals George Thomas (The Rock of Chicamauga), a Virginian, W. T. Sherman, and J. B. McPherson. Grant was promoted to lieutenant general (the first since Washington) and put in charge of all the U.S. armies in the field. He met Lincoln for the first time, moved his headquarters to northern Virginia, and ordered Sherman towards Atlanta. He was ready to take on General Robert E. Lee and the Army of Northern Virginia.

Part II: The Civil War: The Grand Strategies

There was no time during the rebellion when I did not think, and often say, that the South was more to be benefited by its defeat than the North. The latter had the people, the institutions, and the territory to make a great and prosperous nation. The former was burdened with an institution abhorrent to all civilized people not brought up under it, and one which degraded labor, kept it in ignorance and enervated the governing class. With the outside world at war with this institution, they could not have extended their territory. The labor of the country was not skilled nor allowed to become so. The whites could not toil without becoming degraded, and those that did were denominated "poor white trash."
—Memoirs, 1885

I never expect to have an army under my command whipped unless it is very badly whipped and cant help it but I have no idea of being driven to do a desperate or foolish act by the howlings of the press.
—Letter to Jesse Root Grant, April 21, 1863

There were hundreds of battles in the Civil War. It is often hard for lay people or students to follow. The easiest way to understand is to look at the grand strategies of both sides, and then relate the individual battles to the overall strategic goals. After doing this, one can understand the genius of Lincoln, Lee, Grant, and Sherman.

In 1861 the Confederacy wanted to be left alone. It had its own economic and social system, largely based on slavery and the trade of cotton. The rebellion was also partly about states' rights and power in Washington. The free states were developing differently: they had rich farmland and were developing industrially. Many people of the North, and a surprising number in the South, found a system based on slavery morally repugnant, and prospects for the future economically and socially disastrous. When the Confederacy was formed, there was also some inclination to "let the erring sisters go in peace." Lincoln did not think that way. He thought the United States, "the last best hope of man on earth," should remain one nation. Only a war could achieve that, but it would lose much political support if the United States were the aggressor. Some think Lincoln allowed Ft. Sumter, in South Carolina, to become bait, and that the Confederates took the bait, and the war began.

The United States strategy, devised by the then ancient General Winfield

Scott, was the "Anaconda strategy." Like a big constrictor, the United States would cut off the resources of the Confederacy by blockading its ports, surrounding it, and squeezing it. The U. S. Navy was to play a crucial and underpublicized role. Grant and others in the West kept Kentucky in the Union, closed the Mississippi to The Confederacy, and helped win most of Tennessee, a Confederate state with a substantial population loyal to the United States.

Robert E. Lee was an outstanding general, fighting mostly in his home state of Virginia. He outmaneuvered a whole series of United States generals. His job was to protect his home country and punish the United States sufficiently so that European powers would intervene on the side of the Confederacy, or perhaps a divided United States would tire and give up the fight. Grant, a calm and moderate man, thought the newspapers of the United States often undercut the war effort, aiding the cause of the Confederacy.

Lee headed north twice. In 1862 the two sides met at Antietam (a battle involving then Sergeant William McKinley, a future U. S. President) for the bloodiest one-day battle of the war. The United States Army under General McClellan won, partly because a soldier from Indiana found Lee's plans. When the ever cautious McClellan refused to pursue Lee's army, he was removed. Lincoln, waiting for a victory, issued the Emancipation Proclamation, freeing slaves in states still in rebellion. This did not offend the slave states still a part of the United States, but it undercut European leaders whose people generally did not want their nations to support the side of slavery.

In 1863, when Lee again headed north, his goal could have been Harrisburg, Philadelphia, Baltimore, or Washington. The two sides accidentally met at the village of Gettysburg for a three-day battle. The greatest day of the war for the United States was on July 4, 1863, when Lee lost at Gettysburg and Grant conquered Vicksburg. The next year, 1864, was an election year. With all the criticism of the War, it was not clear Lincoln would win. He brought Grant out of the West to face Lee. Grant turned his western army over to Sherman. They agreed Sherman would head to Atlanta, using and destroying resources along the way. Another great general, Phil Sheridan (of Somerset, Ohio) was eventually assigned to operate and destroy the great granary of the Confederacy, the Shenandoah Valley. It was the only way they knew how to win the war. It should be understood that the protracted tragedy of the Civil War was brought about because Confederate troops were highly motivated and Lee, Jackson, Forrest and Joseph E. Johnston were such good generals. They begat the strategies of Grant, Sherman, and Sheridan.

~

Part III: Grant Organizes the U. S. Army for Victory, 1864-1865

Lee's army will be your objective point. Wherever Lee goes there you will go also...
—Letter to Gen. Meade, April 9, 1864

I propose to fight it out along this line if it takes all summer.
—Message to Gen. Halleck from near Spotsylvania Court House, May 11,1864

In Grant's analysis of the military situation in the east in 1864, he thought that the positions of the two armies were similar to what they were in 1861. His solution was to organize as one front the entire United States from the east coast to the Mississippi. Sherman was on the right and would head toward Atlanta from Chattanooga; General Franz Sigel with troops in Virginia and West Virginia was to move in the Shenandoah Valley and one group under General George Crook of the Dayton, Ohio, area (with future presidents, acting Brigadier General Rutherford B. Hayes and acting Captain W. McKinley of the 23rd Ohio) was to leave Charleston, West Virginia, and cut the Virginia and Tennessee Railroad.

The Army of the Potomac, under General Meade but supervised by Grant and located in northern and eastern Virginia, would be the center. The left would be under General Benjamin Butler on the James River in Virginia. All spare troops were to be put on the line, all parts of the line were to attack, and the enemy's resources and supplies were to be destroyed. The Confederacy with Lee, the great general of maneuver, and Joseph E. Johnston, a skilled general, who "lived to fight another day," was to lose its options.

After devastating defeats at Antietam in 1862 and Gettysburg in 1863, at Vicksburg and Chattanooga in the west, and on the seas and rivers, and with Sherman heading for Atlanta, the Confederacy was reeling. Troops as young as 12 and as old as 65 were being recruited, inflation was rampant, cotton was piling up in blockaded ports. The Confederates considered arming slaves, in exchange for their freedom. Lee was mostly in a defensive position; Grant, as he preferred, was attacking.

Grant, the ex-commissary and quartermaster officer, while protecting Washington to the north, kept his back to the east where the United States controlled the mouths of the major rivers in Virginia and thus could supply his huge army. Lee protected Richmond, the Confederate capital. There was a whole series of bloody battles: The Wilderness, Spotsylvania Court House, North Anna, Cold Harbor, Petersburg.

In the west, Sherman marched with three armies from the Chattanooga area towards Atlanta. His campaign culminated in the burning and capture of Atlanta. There was a great loss, however, for Major General McPherson was killed in the battle of Atlanta. McPherson, 35, was the highest ranking U. S. soldier killed in the war. Sherman thought McPherson had the right kind of conciliatory personality and the intellect to become a great political leader. When Grant learned of McPherson's death, he went to his tent and wept. Even John Bell Hood, CSA, a former classmate and then opponent of McPherson, paid him tribute.

McPherson's body was sent home and Sherman headed for Savannah, and then to the Carolinas; Sheridan (with Custer, born New Rumley, Ohio) took over the U.S. Armies in the Shenandoah Valley, conquered, and burned it; Confederate President Jefferson Davis dropped the cautious General Johnston, a general greatly respected by Grant, and replaced him with the aggressive General John Bell Hood, who headed for Sherman's supply base in Tennessee. Hood's army was decimated by those of Generals John Schofield and George Thomas. Grant dumped two inept political generals, Banks and Butler, and captured the port of Wilmington, North Carolina. Grant conceded there were mistakes made in his campaign against Lee, and it is difficult to call many of the battles victories, but generally Lee lost supplies and men and moved his lines back. Meanwhile Sherman's army was exerting pressure from the south.

After the U. S. Army captured Petersburg, Virginia, Lee abandoned Richmond. Grant had him chased. Sheridan's cavalry and infantry under the "Boy General," Nelson A. Miles, blocked Lee's way. Lee's troops were boxed in and he surrendered at Appomattox. At Appomattox Lee was neat and handsome and courtly. Grant wore his usual private's uniform with his general's stars tacked on. He had been out riding with his troops and he was dirty. The terms of surrender were generous, reflecting the ideas of both Lincoln and Grant. Later that month Johnston surrendered to Sherman, and effectively the War was over.

~

Part IV: How Did Grant Become a Great General?

Some of our generals failed because they worked everything out by rule. They knew what Frederick did at one place and Napoleon at another. They were always thinking about what Napoleon would do. Unfortunately for their plans, the rebels would be thinking about something else....

—U. S. Grant

The bloody nature of Shiloh impressed itself on Grant.

(Grant) sees every failure a fresh incentive to further action. His reticence at this moment is truly heroic; it is work and not failure which absorbs him. Nothing unhinges him or weakens his faith in himself and final victory. He soars above his subordinates, forgetting their mistakes so that he may waste not a moment...If he cannot destroy Lee, then he will destroy his communications; if he cannot destroy his communications, then he will invest Petersburg. Though means vary, his idea remains constant....

—J. F. C. Fuller, *The Generalship of Ulysses S. Grant*

Greatness is not accidental, nor is it inevitable. It is the right person at the right time having the right qualities. U. S. Grant was the greatest general on the winning side of the Civil War. He was a quiet, often unkempt person with modest ambitions that never seemed to work out. At West Point he was acknowledged to be the greatest horseman there. He was intuitive with animals and people. He was objective, strong in math and drawing, and had common sense. Often forgotten about Grant is that he was a lover of literature and travel. He was curious about people and places, always learning. At West Point, Grant appears to be the classic unmotivated student, gaining demerits for what he thought were insipid rules. He failed generally to impress professors, yet did impress some of his most astute fellow students.

After receiving four years of free education at West Point, Grant served in the Army because he felt a personal obligation. His fate was to be in the infantry. More flamboyant officers like Sheridan, Custer, Stuart, and Forrest would be cavalry officers. In the infantry, Grant was not appointed as a leader of men but an organizer of supplies and logistics, as a quartermaster or commissary officer. Grant was a hard worker and learned this job well. More intellectual or arrogant officers might have been contemptuous of such a function. In the Civil War Grant used his knowledge to supply an army of 100,000 or more.

During the Mexican War, Grant observed two great generals, Zachary Taylor and Winfield Scott, and dealt more informally with a leader of volunteers and future president, Franklin Pierce. Taylor was an informal general possessed of great common sense and personal courage. Scott, the epitome of a regular army officer, violated military theory by cutting his own supply lines and living off the land, taking a relatively small army (including Marines) from the port city of Vera Cruz to the "Halls of Montezuma" in Mexico City, where he attacked an entrenched army in its own land. Grant was particularly impressed with Scott's use of engineers (his lead engineer was Robert E. Lee) to dislodge defenders in an often mountainous area. When peace came, Grant was impressed with Scott's generous terms. It was consistent with his own.

In the Mexican War Grant did his supply work, but when battles came he fought with the front line troops. As always he was courageous, resourceful, and quiet. Some officers were boastful, pointing out what they had done. Characteristically, Grant never did this, which is one reason his peers always respected him. Eventually he received three awards for his courage, making him a 1st lieutenant and a brevet captain. (He would be appointed captain when an appropriate vacancy occurred.) Grant enjoyed the company of Pierce, a decent and likable man. Grant thought the Mexican War was wrong, started by President Polk and others to expand slavery. He also thought Polk (and Washington, DC) played games with Taylor and Scott, both of whom were Whigs and both of whom would eventually run for President. Grant had great sympathy with the ordinary Mexican people. He thought they were badly misled by cynical and selfish leaders, just as he thought that the blacks and lower class whites of the slave states were. Later he sympathized with American Indians and the Chinese. Grant was not a great political theorist, but his normal generosity was enlightened by a fundamental understanding of American principles of freedom and equality.

Finally Grant, the informal officer, always worked with the common soldier. They were often uneducated, from the farms and hollows of America, or foreign countries like Ireland or Germany. He found many had common sense and he used it. Later, as a colonel or a general, he saw their talents and resourcefulness and always thought his army was unbeatable. This he communicated to the soldiers and they believed him. As Lincoln was a President with great empathy for the common man, Grant had great empathy with the common soldier—a soldier's general.

In terms of communications, if Ambrose Bierce, Grant's compatriot and fellow soldier from Meigs County, Ohio, is right and "clear writing is good thinking made visible," Grant should be ranked among the best of thinkers. His letters are available from his West Point years on. Although the spelling can be faulted, there is nothing unclear in any of his messages. While some generals wrote for history, or to cover themselves should things go wrong, Grant wrote simple, terse, straightforward messages. His subordinates would have a difficult time claiming they didn't understand his orders. When he had to drop political or other incompetent generals, the written word supported him.

~

Part V. Grant and Politics, 1865-1880

It was my fortune, or misfortune, to be called to the office of Chief Executive without any previous political training. Under such circumstances, it is reasonable to suppose that errors of judgment must have occurred...
 —Memoirs, 1885

Just as there were seeds of greatness in Grant prior to the Civil War, there were also seeds of failure for his role as a political leader. From at least the days of the Mexican War, the intuitive Grant had an aversion to Washington. The straight-forward, generous, trusting soldier would suffer his greatest defeats in politics. Why did he get involved? After Lincoln's death, with hatred in the air, he stifled his normal qualms, probably thinking there was room in Washington for common sense, generosity, and compassion. But his reputation was nearly destroyed there. His fellow general, W. T. Sherman, whose brother, John, was almost nominated for president, was more forceful: "I will not accept if nominated, I will not serve if elected." Grant should have said the same.

Lincoln invited the Grants to attend Ford's Theater on April 14, 1865. The Grants liked the theater, but Julia Grant probably didn't want to deal with the sometimes unpleasant Mrs. Lincoln, and Grant, always the family man, was eager to see his children in New Jersey. Had he gone, Grant might have died that night, or he might have saved Lincoln's life.

The assassination of Lincoln was an insane act, causing incalculable harm to the country, South and North. It was our most difficult period of history. Deaths from the war exceeded 600,000, more than our total losses from World Wars I and II combined, or roughly *ten* times the number that died in Vietnam. The soldiers Grant, Lee, Sherman, and Johnston, wanted peace. Lincoln's policy was to be "...malice toward none, with charity for all...." When he died the policy didn't have a chance. Loud-mouthed men of hatred, North and South, took over. Andrew Johnson of Tennessee, the new President, who had remained loyal to the United States although his state had seceded, had some virtues, but he was not equal to the task. Secretary of War Stanton (born Steubenville, Ohio, graduated Kenyon College) and many others were convinced that the Lincoln assassination had been a Confederate plot.

Vengeance was called for. Ironically General Sherman got caught in the political crossfire. He and Grant had met with Lincoln. They had understood the kind of peace that Lincoln wanted. When he offered it to Joseph Johnston and his army, Sherman was repudiated by President Johnson, Secretary Stanton, and the Congress. Sherman was insulted and Grant was caught in the middle. They had to renegotiate the surrender with Johnston. Grant, the nation's top general, just wanted to do his job. He demobilized the army and sent soldiers under General Sheridan to the Mexican border where the French leader, Napoleon III, had taken advantage of the American Civil War by setting up Emperor Maximilian, an Austrian and Empress Carlotta, (Charlotte), a Belgian. They fell to the forces of Benito Juarez, Maximilian was executed, and Carlotta went insane, ending the crises for the United States.

Reconstruction was another difficult period in our history, second only to the war. At home, Lee was indicted for his actions against the United States. Grant thought such an indictment violated the surrender terms, and threatened to resign. The indictment was quietly dropped. The governments of the former Confederate and some border states had been dominated by slave-holding planters. The state laws and economic systems were designed to favor them. They led their states to secession, which, in turn, led to war. There were, especially in upland areas, many whites who did not support slavery, secession, or the War. They had more in common with the independent farmers of Pennsylvania, Ohio, and Indiana than the slave owning planters of the south. The difference was that they had much less power and influence. Many, especially Kentuckians and Tennesseeans, fought for the United States in the Civil War. Western Virginians seceded from Virginia and formed a new state. East Tennesseeans talked of doing the same.

Unfortunately, while many of the conquerors sought reconciliation, the planters of the South regained control of the governments. They abolished slavery, as required by the 13th Amendment, but instituted "black codes," to take freedom and economic rights away from the newly freed slaves. In the North, there was a group of Radical Republicans who believed that southern leaders should be punished. There was malice everywhere. President Andrew Johnson, an inept politician, got caught in the middle. His vetoes of Civil Rights Acts, failure to protect the freedmen of the South, and attempts to violate the overreaching *Tenure of Office Act* led to his impeachment. He was narrowly acquitted but finished politically.

~

Part VI. Grant as President

General Grant...I think he had better let well enough alone. He makes a good general, but I should think a very poor President.
        —Mary Todd Lincoln est. 1868

In 1868 the country, tired of the bickering and partisanship, turned to a non-politician, Grant. Like Hoover in the 1920's and Eisenhower in 1958, Grant was not strongly identified with a political party. He had voted for Buchanan in 1856 and Douglas in 1860, both Democrats. Lincoln had been a great supporter of Grant during the War, and Grant supported him in 1864. If it had not been for Johnson, who sought the Democratic nomination in 1868, Grant might have been nominated as a Democrat. Grant did not campaign and made few promises. His theme was, "Let us have Peace."

Grant's political ideas were few and simple. He thought the Lincoln policy of malice towards none was right. They shared the same natural generosity of spirit.

He was concerned with the plight of the most helpless: the Mexican peon, American Indians, Chinese railroad workers, the ex-slaves and the poor whites. He was also for sound money. Unlike Lincoln, he was not clever politically.

In terms of personnel, Grant would probably have used McPherson, one of the brightest and most politically sensitive of his generals whose loss to the country was inestimable. Early in Grant's first term there was another tragedy for Grant, and probably the country. His best friend, advisor, and the individual frequently cited as Grant's conscience, John A. Rawlins, died of consumption (tuberculosis). Rawlins was intelligent and objective, and Grant, a man with a narrow circle of close friends, listened to him. He could warn Grant about bad decisions and connivers. Unfortunately, Grant was surrounded by connivers, some of whom were from his own, or his wife Julia's family.

Grant had a mixed record as President. There was not only the hatred and bitterness of the Reconstruction process but westward expansion and attendant conflicts with American Indians, and there was the industrialization of America with few standards for conflicts of interests but opportunities for financial chicanery at all levels of society. In 1868 the Republican party was ascendant and unchallenged. When any political party gains such a position, many of the worst elements gain positions of power.

The scandals started during the Civil War when suppliers, often well connected to politicians, sold shoddy goods to the U. S. Army. As a general, Grant fought local suppliers of substandard goods, which probably was to the detriment of his career. After the war, there was the Tweed ring in New York; "Boss" Shepherd in Washington, and the greatest of all scandals, *Credit Mobilier,* a construction company set up to skim money out of the Union Pacific railroad, which in turn billed the Federal Government for expenses. That scandal ultimately implicated many members of Congress, including the former speaker of the house and Grant's first vice president, Schulyer Colfax of Indiana. Grant had nothing to do with any of these scandals.

The scandals for which Grant gets blamed began early. In 1869 two speculators, Jim Fisk and Jay Gould, tried to rig the gold market. They had formed a business relationship with one of Grant's brothers-in-law, Abel Corbin, and may have involved other family members or close friends of Grant. As the price of gold soared, Grant and his Secretary of Treasury became aware of the plot. They sold *Federal* gold to increase the supply. On September 24, 1869—Black Friday—this dropped the price precipitously and ruined many speculators, including Corbin. Other scandals included a tax collection scandal involving a payment to a specially commissioned agent of a contingent fee of fifty percent of the taxes collected; the Whiskey Ring, involving bribes to hundreds of Federal officials, probably including Orville Babcock, a former staff officer and associate of Grant; and the Belknap scandal, involving bribes to the Secretary of War (and his wife) for the award of trading posts at Indian reservations.

Grant hired an honest attorney general, Benjamin Bristow of Kentucky, to go after the crooks but later influenced by Babcock, who seemed to be able to manipulate Grant, Grant became obtuse, giving only lukewarm support to Bristow. He also appointed good men to key positions like Alfonso Taft (father of future President and Chief Justice, William Howard Taft) and Jacob Cox (of Warren, Ohio) and Hamilton Fish, as well as Belknap and Babcock. In the meanwhile, Congress was running things. Government appointments were made on the basis of patronage, and many of the most corrupt and incompetent were hired.

There were two main factions of Republicans in Congress. The worst faction, the Stalwarts, were led by Roscoe Conkling of New York, Simeon Cameron of Pennsylvania, and Benjamin Butler (the incompetent Civil War general) of Massachusetts. The reformers were led by Carl Schurz, Charles Sumner, Horace Greeley, and John Quincy Adams's son, Charles Francis Adams. Both factions vied for Grant's support. When Sumner and Schurz failed to support Grant on the repeal of *The Tenure of Office Act*, Grant was pushed into the arms of the Stalwarts. Although political hacks in many ways, they proved to be more practical than the reformers. R. B. Hayes, a shrewd observer and future President, looked at his party and said, in effect, that the good were not clever, and the clever were not good.

Unfortunately, the Stalwarts got Grant reelected in 1872. The reform Republicans, joined later by the Democrats, picked a loser in newspaperman Horace Greeley, a talented writer and editor who had been on many sides of many issues. Early in the second term, the failure of Jay Cooke and Company led to the Panic of 1873, a major depression. (Cooke, born in Sandusky, Ohio, working with Treasury Secretary Salmon P. Chase of Cincinnati, had been a financial hero of the Civil War.) Grant was willing to run again in 1876, and in 1880. The Republican party picked the morally upright war hero, Rutherford B. Hayes, in 1876 and the well-educated James A. Garfield in 1880.

Grant's presidency had some positive achievements. He supported the Fourteenth and Fifteenth Amendments to the Constitution, and supported and had civil rights acts passed. He appointed Amos Akerman of Georgia, a genuine hero, to enforce civil rights in the South. He appointed Ely S. Parker, an American

Indian, as commissioner of Indian affairs. He arranged for the settlement of *Alabama* claims, claims for damage to the United States by British-built ships used by the Confederacy. And despite Congress, he got the first civil service law passed.

For one solution to the problem of ex-slaves in the South he proposed the annexation of Santo Domingo (Dominican Republic). He thought many could migrate there and have full rights as American citizens and, in turn, this would put pressure on the South to try to retain its labor force by treating blacks better. The concept was blocked by Senator Charles Sumner who wanted to annex parts of Canada. Grant also had the first surveys made for a canal across Central America.

Grant's greatest failures as President were not having the follow-through he showed in the Civil War, not following his own instincts, and listening to the wrong people. This is probably because his political objectives and his knowledge of how to achieve them were not as clear as his military objectives. No doubt he also suffered the loss of Rawlings, an honest voice in a deceitful world, who would have reminded him who he was and what he was for. Finally there was the difficulty of the times and the high expectations for Grant. Who knows how the great Lincoln, one of our cleverest political operators, would have coped? In 1877, hampered by the economic depression, the scandals, the Stalwart Republicans, and advisors like Babcock, Grant left the presidency.

After leaving office, the Grants made an around-the-world tour. They met Queen Victoria, Bismarck, and the rulers of Japan and China. Grant was especially inspired by a parade and celebration in Newcastle-on-Tyne in England where thousands of workmen and ordinary citizens greeted him as a hero. The Grants came home in time for him to barely lose the Republican nomination for President in 1880.

~

Part VII. Final Tragedy and Transcendence

I do not sleep, although sometimes I dose off a little. If up I am talked to and my efforts to answer cause pain. The fact is I think I am a verb instead of a personal pronoun. A verb is any thing that signifies to be; to do; or to suffer. I signify all three.
  —U. S. Grant, July 1885

Grant fought to remain alive and complete his memoirs, finishing them a week before his death.

After briefly returning to Galena, the Grants moved in 1881 to New York City. They had gotten used to the good life, and he decided to become a businessman and investor. Unfortunately he was manipulated by both friends and family. He invested his money in Grant and Ward, a firm involving his son and a fast and loose, somewhat charismatic banker named Ferdinand Ward. Ward used the same collateral several times and did very well until times turned bad (the depression of 1884) and he couldn't pay all the firm's debts. He went to Grant who borrowed $150,000 from William Henry Vanderbilt. It wasn't enough, the bank failed, and Ward fled the country. This was humiliating to Grant who paid Vanderbilt back by giving him all his Civil War items and gifts from citizens around the world. Vanderbilt eventually turned everything over to the Smithsonian.

At 62, Grant was broke again. It was suggested that he write magazine articles on his Civil War experiences, which were a commercial and literary success. And this led to the suggestion that he write his personal memoirs. The task became urgent when Grant, a cigar smoker since his Civil War days, learned that he had cancer of the soft palate and esophagus.

Grant's last battle was to finish the *Memoirs* before death. There are pictures of him in his final months: pale, weak, often doped by cocaine for the pain and morphine to sleep, writing, dictating until he can no longer speak, writing again. In March, he coughed, hemorrhaged, and nearly died. Surprisingly, it is now thought he probably lost tissue and cancer cells, which cleared his breathing passages. He got better and wrote on. He finished the book in July. Published by a company set up by Mark Twain, the memoirs became one of the great books of American literature, a simple, clear, straight-forward, intelligent and sometimes humble explication of the life of U.S. Grant from his Ohio beginnings through the Civil War. It earned his estate a major fortune at the time: $450,000.

●**Deaths:** Ulysses S. Grant died in Mount McGregor, New York, July 23, 1885. Julia Dent Grant lived on, mostly in Washington, until December 14, 1902. She wrote her memoirs in 1890, but they were not published until 1975. The Grants are buried in Grant's Tomb in New York City. The tomb has been neglected and trashed, and there is some hope the family would consent to their bodies being moved back to southern Ohio.

●**The Land of Grant Tour**

The house in which Grant was born can be visited in Point Pleasant, Ohio, about 25 miles east of Cincinnati, on U.S. 52. Grant went to one school in Ripley, Ohio, about 25 miles east. The Rankin house and the John P. Parker house, both national landmarks, connected with the "underground railroad" are also there. It is believed that the Rankin house was used as a model for a house that gave Eliza shelter in *Uncle Tom's Cabin*, the most important book of the 1850s and 1860s. (Harriet Beecher Stowe lived in Cincinnati from 1852-1860.)

Grant's main home while he was growing up is in Georgetown, about ten miles northwest of Ripley on U.S. 68. It is a national monument. (Both houses are near creeks, necessary for the tanning business.) Finally, both the Grant family and the Simpson family had connections to Bethel, Ohio, ten miles west of Georgetown. The entire tour can easily be done in one day from Cincinnati or Dayton.

Grant's boyhood home and the tannery in Georgetown, Ohio.

●Works Relevant to Understanding the Grants

A. Biographical

Grant's unusually dramatic life has led many to write about him in both the nineteenth and twentieth centuries. Most concede that Grant was smart rather than lucky during the Civil War and was indeed a great general. They differ on his political failings on extent and causes. Other works are useful to understand his times and character.

●◆Catton, Bruce.

This Oberlin graduate and masterful writer on the Civil War wrote three books on Grant all published by Little Brown and Company, Boston, MA:

U. S. Grant and the American Military Tradition; 1954
This is a concise over view of U.S. Grant's career. The other two are more thorough and dramatic accounts of the Civil War.

Grant Moves South; 1960
Grant Takes Command; 1969

◆◆**Fuller, J. F. C.** 1929. *The Generalship of Ulysses S. Grant,* reprinted 1958; New York: De Capo Press.

Fuller was a British general and a student of military history. He makes the case that Grant, a man with "reasoned clairvoyance," was the greatest strategic general of the Civil War, who intuitively understood and supported Lincoln's objectives, who thought of any setbacks as only temporary, and who inspired his troops with his common sense, rather than charisma.

◆◆**Grant, Julia Dent.** (Written in the 1890's, published in 1975). *Personal Memoirs.* New York: G. P. Putnam's Sons.

Although this book has far too much on their trip around the world, it has good insights on both Ulysses and Julia.

◆◆**Grant Ulysses S.** 1885. *Personal Memoirs.* (Often reprinted, one current edition 1990). New York: Literary Classics of America, Inc.

This is Grant in his own words, justifiably a literary classic, a clear easy-to-read book showing both sophistication and humility. Unfortunately it covers the period only through his military career.

◆◆**Hesseltine, William B.** 1935. *U. S. Grant, Politician.* New York: Dodd, Mead & Company.

This is a psychological study of the character of Grant. Son of a contentious father, Grant developed a suppressed personality that dealt much better with animals than people. Grant floated through life but was inspired by major challenges to which he brought a practical mind, if a kind of a trial and error method. He learned well from his errors and never made the same mistake twice. As President, Grant was immediately offended by "reformers" like Schurz and Sumner, by their failure to support him on the repeal of the *Tenure in Office Act.* Sumner further offended by failing to support Grant on the annexation of Santo Domingo. Moreover, Sumner's speaking style was cruel and contemptuous, certain to offend a man as sensitive as Grant. Grant made it his goal to get rid of Sumner, and he did. To do this he cozied up to the worst elements in his party, the Stalwart Republicans like Conkling and Butler, and became a regular party man. His great mandate from the people evaporated.

Lewis, Lloyd. 1950. *Captain Sam Grant.* Boston: Little, Brown and Co.

This is a good book covering Grant's early years. Unfortunately Lewis, who wrote the classic, *Sherman, Fighting Prophet,* died before completing a comprehensive three-volume biography on Grant.

McFeely, William S. 1981. *Grant A Biography.* W. W. Norton & Company, New York: W. W. Norton & Company.

This is a somewhat complicated book. Its theses include that Grant rose to clear-cut challenges in war and in his final task. After the Civil War he (and Mrs. Grant) learned to love the adulation of the crowds, and Grant obsessively feared returning to the days of failure after he first left the army. It tends to agree with the Hesseltine theory that Grant as a political leader was captured by the Stalwarts because he was put off by the moralistic and sanctimonious tone of the reform Republicans, mainly by Charles Sumner of Massachusetts.

B. Non-Biographical

Dreiser, Theodore. 1912. *The Financier.* New York. A Signet Classic, New American Library.

This book, written by a former newspaperman and set mostly in the 1870s and 1880s vividly illustrates the capitalism of the day.

Foner, Eric. 1990. *A Short History of Reconstruction 1863-1877.* New York. Harper & Row.

Reconstruction was one of the most tragic, misunderstood, purposely misconstrued periods of American history. Foner has written a clear, generally fair, and objective account of this complex period. It underlines the tragic loss of Lincoln, the unconscious ineptitude of Andrew Johnson, the cautious pragmatism of Grant, and the cynical manipulations of southern planters who having led their states into disunion and war sought to reinstate slavery in all but name. It covers "Black Codes," and the inevitable reaction of Radical Republicans who were in many ways responsible for the Thirteenth, Fourteenth, and Fifteenth Amendments. Finally it puts into context the election of Hayes, who like so many veterans of the Civil War, thought the victory in the war would be lost if the Democrats were allowed to triumph in 1876.

●**Hugo, Victor.** 1862. *Les Miserables.* Available in many editions.

U. S. Grant, former head of the literary club at West Point, and Julia Dent Grant, remained interested in literature all their lives. In her memoirs, Julia tells of recommending this book to her husband on their trip home from Japan. He picked it up, read it obsessively, pronouncing it a great book.

●**James, Henry.** 1878. *Daisy Miller.* (This is a novelette, widely available in anthologies or short works of Henry James).

The personality of Daisy, a vivacious American, encountering the world of Europe, with tragic results, was supposedly modeled on "first daughter" Nellie Grant, whose well-publicized White House marriage to a wealthy Englishman ended in failure.

●**Shakespeare, William.** 1599 (est.). *Julius Caesar.*

The "noblest Roman of them all," was Brutus who had the ability to see things objectively, and the inclination to act for the greater good. In many ways the character of Rawlins paralleled that of Brutus.

●*Othello;* 1604 (est.)

Othello was a soldier. His tragedy was brought about because he listened to Iago. It was similar the way Grant listened to Babcock, who shared war experiences with Grant, but who impressed no one other than Grant.

●**Thoreau, Henry David.** 1846-1862. *On Civil Disobedience.* Available with Thoreau essays.

While Thoreau was at Walden pond writing his great book, America was going to war with Mexico. This was his protest, compiled originally as a speech in 1846. It was published later after Thoreau's death in 1862.

●**Twain, Mark.** 1917. *Autobiography.* edited by Charles Neider in 1959. New York: Harper and Row.

This is an autobiography pieced together after Twain's death. As one would expect, it is full of entertaining anecdotes from Twain's earliest days in Missouri through fame and fortune (sometimes) in the New York publishing world. Grant, though taciturn, impressed Twain. Twain was a prodigious reader and he classified Grant's *Memoirs* with Caesar's *Commentaries* as among the greatest military books written.

Rutherford Birchard Hayes

Civilized and Rational

19th President
March 4, 1877–March 4, 1881

Sometimes a cause is so powerful that it impels thousands, or even millions, to disrupt their lives. Such a cause was the Civil War. Rutherford B. Hayes was one who joined the cause. At age 38 the sociable and literary Hayes was comfortable. He had built a successful law practice, had a charming wife and a growing family. The Hayes's social life was based on things they cared about—good company and ideas. But ideas are empty if not practiced. To Hayes the Civil War was about the greatest political ideas—keeping the country together and freeing the slaves. He dropped everything to follow Lincoln and go off to war. In the war he was recklessly courageous, being wounded five times. He missed the great battle of Antietam because he was seriously wounded at South Mountain. When he came home a hero, others put him into office. There he did what he thought was right.

I am a radical in thought (and principle) and a conservative in method (and conduct).
　　—Diary, December 12, 1890

◄ *Hayes: a quiet but determined reformer in the White House*

Our government has been called the white man's government. Not so. It is not the government of any class, sect, nationality or race. It is the government founded on the consent of the governed.

—Speech at Lebanon, Ohio, August 5, 1867

●**Family Heritage:** Hayes was born October 4, 1822, in Delaware, Ohio, son of Sophie Birchard and Rutherford Hayes. The Hayes's were New Englanders whose ancestors came from Scotland (1680) and England to Connecticut. Hayes's father was born in Brattleboro, Vermont, and worked as a merchant in Wilmington and Dummerstown, Vermont. His mother was from Wilmington, Vermont, and both the Hayeses and the Birchards were related to accomplished New England families. Visiting his many relatives in New England, Hayes generally found the females of his family much stronger and more intelligent than the males. One worrisome factor was a family pattern of insanity. Hayes's father died before he was born. Later his nine- year-old brother died while ice skating. Young Hayes was raised in a protective manner by his mother, her husband's spinster sister, and to a slight extent by his mother's intractable bachelor brother, Sardis Birchard. Sardis Birchard had been raised by the Hayeses when his parents died. He would become the surrogate father of Hayes and later leave substantial property and money to Hayes. Hayes was also extremely close to a sister, Fanny, who was two years older than he. Fanny was very bright and loving. She and Hayes, while respecting their mother and her demanding rules, learned to evade them in a non-threatening way.

Careful men like you should not encourage extravagance in Ohio when there is so much need for money for Preachers and Teachers to instruct the ignorant that are so plenty around us. The character of the inhabitants is much more important than their style of living.

—Sophia B. Hayes to her brother Sardis Birchard in reaction to his plans for building of what would become the Hayes house in Fremont, March 30, 1860

●**Religion:** Sophie Birchard Hayes was a religious Presbyterian; her favorite book was John Bunyan's *Pilgrim's Progress.* Lucy Webb, who became Hayes's wife, was a Methodist with strong anti-slavery and anti-alcohol views. Hayes greatly respected those views. Although Hayes attended many churches, he did not join any. He had difficulties with the creeds and probably disliked their often petty factionalism. He was an admirer of William Ellery Channing and Ralph Waldo Emerson and was probably closest in beliefs to Unitarianism.

●**Education:** Hayes, always a reader, attended private school as a youth in Delaware and Norwalk, Ohio, and Middletown, Connecticut. At age 16 he attended Kenyon College in Gambier, Ohio, where he studied liberal arts. He graduated first in his class and made several lifelong friends. After a year of reading law in Columbus, Hayes went to Harvard Law School from which he graduated in 1845. He also learned German so that he might be able to represent some of the numerous German-speaking immigrants then in Ohio.

●**Wife:** Hayes married Lucy Ware Webb, December 30, 1852, in Cincinnati. Lucy was born August 28, 1831, in Chillicothe, Ohio, later moving to Delaware, Ohio, and then Cincinnati. Her father, James Webb, a Chillicothe physician, died when she was an infant. Lucy was one of the first women to attend Ohio Wesleyan, later graduated from Wesleyan College in Cincinnati, and became the first First Lady

Lucy: one of the best-loved First Ladies

to be a college graduate. Lucy was exceptional: kind, generous, perceptive. She became one of the most beloved first ladies in the nineteenth century. Her encouragement of the banning of alcohol at White House functions caused her later to be dubbed "Lemonade Lucy." The Hayeses had eight children, including four sons and a daughter that survived infancy.

●**Personal characteristics:** Hayes had auburn hair and a ruddy complexion and was given the nickname of Rud. He became the epitome of a nineteenth century gentleman. He was kind, respectful, and affable, with a great gift for friendship with people at all levels. This made him a good leader of troops and trustworthy as a political leader. In contrast to some nineteenth century leaders, Hayes wrote and spoke simple and clear English. In his feelings for common people, Hayes was one of the truest heirs to Lincoln.

~

Part I: Early Life

Sophia Birchard Hayes's early life was difficult. Her father died when she was thirteen, her mother and older sister and brother died when she was twenty. She lost a daughter at age four, her husband at age 36, and a son—"a perfect boy" who tragically drowned in an ice skating accident at age 9. She was left with two children, her independent brother, a younger sister, and her faith. She sought to protect the children from disease and accident. The children, Fanny and Rutherford (Rud), grew up to be avid readers and observers and hard workers. They also learned to enjoy people and have fun.

Rutherford liked school and was a good student, but when he was out of school he liked to relax, hunt, and fish. Sometimes, he questioned the value of education. His mother, sister, aunt, and even uncle questioned his ambition.

...the ignorant farm boy is happier than the student...
   —Rud, age 14

...the literary man has a thousand joys the rustic never has...
   —Fanny, age 16

At the school in Middletown and Kenyon College there were many rules, but Hayes learned to bend or break them without getting into serious troubles. Kenyon's entire senior class walked out in protest of a disciplinary action. Sophia Hayes gained gray hair, but Hayes knew that it would not look good for Kenyon if no seniors graduated, and he was right: the administration backed down. When graduation was restored, Hayes was the valedictorian.

After college Hayes read law in Columbus. He also studied German so he could represent some of the many German-speaking residents of Ohio. Reading law wasn't very stimulating, and Hayes and his family decided he should go off to Boston to study law at Harvard under Judge Joseph Story and Simon Greenleaf. While at Harvard he voted in his first presidential election, supporting Henry Clay the Whig but betting and winning on James K. Polk, the Democrat.

I must keep a guard on my susceptibles, or I shall be beyond of my depth.
　　—On dealing with women, May 4, 1850

The mystery of our existence—I have no faith in any attempted explanation of it. It is all dark, unfathomed, profound.
　　—On the death of his cousin, Sarah Wasson, October 24, 1850

Initially Hayes practiced law in Lower Sandusky (Fremont). His uncle was an important businessman in town and could steer business his way. His mother wanted him closer to home, then in Columbus, and his sister thought he should practice law in a more sophisticated place. Hayes himself became bored and decided to head to Cincinnati.

Before the Civil War, Cincinnati was the most dynamic city in the West. Hayes had a surprising number of friends there. He and several friends formed the Cincinnati Literary Society to meet weekly and talk about books. His law practice started slowly. He entered a partnership with a politically connected lawyer. He got his chance with a couple of murder cases and a fugitive slave case. On the *Nancy Farrer* case he pleaded insanity for her and had her conviction thrown out on appeal. He volunteered to take fugitive slave cases and participated in the *Rosetta Armstead* case, which made him locally famous. Later he was elected Cincinnati city solicitor.

It is no use doubting or rolling it over in my thoughts. By George! I am in love with her.
　　—Written about Lucy Ware Webb, June 14, 1851

Hayes was popular with girls. However, although he respected his mother and was close to his sister, he was generally much more comfortable with men than with women. At age 24 he proposed to a woman from Connecticut and she accepted, but they broke up over the issue as to where they would live. His mother picked out for him the young daughter of one of her friends, Lucy Ware

Webb, who had lived in both Delaware and Cincinnati. Hayes, thinking she was far too young, didn't pay much attention to her. He had unsuccessful romances with three or four others. He called on Lucy at college when she was 18. Lucy was different, less sophisticated than the big city girls, more natural. She was quick-witted, cheerful and a lover of music, with a nice alto voice. They talked about literature, laughed, and had fun. Hayes pursued sophisticated city girls but returned to Lucy. Gradually he discovered he loved her. Every one approved of Lucy: his mother, his uncle, his sister, and his friends.

A better wife I never hoped to have....This is indeed life....Blessings on his head who first invented marriage.
　　　—Hayes Diary, February 27, 1853

In 1854 the Hayeses had the first of their eight children, their finances were improving, and they moved into a new house. Hayes became one of the founders of the Republican party and met with Lincoln. But tragedy struck the family again when his beloved sister, Fanny Platt, died in childbirth.

My dear only sister, my beloved Fanny is dead! The dearest friend of childhood...
the confidante of all my life, the one I loved best is gone. I can recall no happiness in the past
which was not brightened either by her participation in it or the thought of her joy
when she knew of it. All plans for the future, all visions of success have embraced her....
For many years, my mother's family consisted of but three....Oh what associations now cling
around those tender early days!...My heart bleeds and tears flow as I write.
　　　—Letter to Guy M. Bryan, July 23, 1856

Hayes would never forget Fanny. But his life was soon to change dramatically.

I feel as if the time had come when to test this question. If the threats are meant,
then it is time the Union was dissolved, or the traitors crushed out.
　　　—Diary, November 6, 1860

The Hayeses's happy domestic life: Lucy invited children to roll Easter eggs on the White House lawn. ▶

~

Part II: Hayes in the Civil War

*I would prefer to go into it (the Civil War) if I knew I was to die, or be killed
in the course of it, than to live through and after without taking any part in it.*
  —Diary, May 15, 1861

*How the manly, generous, brave side of our people is growing. With all its evils,
war has its glorious compensations.*
  —Letter to his mother, March 6, 1862

The deadliest enemy the Union has is slavery—in fact it is the only enemy.
  —Diary, May 31, 1862

*Fighting battles is like courting the girls: those who make the most pretensions
and are boldest usually win.*
  —Letter to Sardis Birchard, August 6, 1862

When he became aware that there was going to be a Civil War, Hayes and his
colleague and fellow lawyer, Stanley Matthews of Cincinnati, signed up as volunteers. The states remaining loyal to the United States were raising volunteer
regiments who, contrary to military custom, usually elected their own officers.
For the 23rd Ohio Regiment, consisting of about 1,000 men from northern and
northwest Ohio, Governor William Dennison appointed Hayes as major and
Matthews as lieutenant colonel. The initial colonel for the regiment was a West
Point graduate and army drop-out, William Rosecrans, who later became a well-
known general. The 23rd also had an 18-year-old private, William McKinley,
who would later become corporal, sergeant, lieutenant, captain, brevet major, and
finally President of the United States.

The concept of voluntary regiments with elected or politically appointed officers is a uniquely American institution. Hayes learned military procedures and
tactics from West Pointers and the rest from books. There was often tension
between the West Pointers and the volunteers. The former were imbued with
their own special language and procedures, desiring to give unquestioned orders.
The volunteers were civilians in uniforms, from a practical society, and wanted to
understand *why* they should do things.

Hayes, who became colonel and regimental leader in 1862, was their ideal

Hayes (at left) fought bravely in the war, was wounded several times, and much beloved by his men.

leader. He understood the West Point emphasis on drill and conditioning. He learned how a regiment (1,000 men) would fit in with a brigade (3,000-4,000 men), a division (10,000-12,000 men) and a corps (two-three divisions). He also understood that West Pointers could impose stupid and arbitrary rules. When he could, Hayes fought such rules. He came to treat the men of the 23rd as family, the same way Sardis Birchard had treated him (and Hayes's parents treated Sardis Birchard). There became a kind of mystical emotional bond between leader and troops that few of them ever forgot. Using his lawyerly skills he taught the men of the 23rd rules and tactics and the reasons for them. When battles came (more than 50 times) he didn't point to an objective and say *"you* take it," he led them. Hayes was wounded or injured five times, had three horses shot from under him, and once was reported dead. Upon visiting her husband, Lucy Webb Hayes served as a voluntary nurse to the many wounded, often returning in tears.

The 23rd was initially assigned to protect the Baltimore and Ohio Railroad line, which ran from Washington to Cincinnati in northwestern Virginia. (This part of Virginia became West Virginia in 1863.) Like Kentucky and Tennessee, it was considered strategic and held many sympathizers for the United States. The war-time conditions were difficult with lots of marching up mountains and through valleys. The year 1862 was rainy with mud and flooding adding to their difficulties. Hayes and the 23rd fought a series of small battles. This and the challenging physical conditions served as a great learning experience, toughening them up. Hayes thought the 23rd became a top-notch regiment, and all their commanding generals, assigning them the most difficult jobs, seemed to agree.

Give them hell! Give the sons of bitches hell!
    —Hayes, before the Battle of South Mountain, in Maryland,
September 14, 1862

When in 1862 Lee threatened the North by crossing the Potomac, the 23rd and most of the army in western Virginia was called to attack at South Mountain and Antietam in Maryland. The army, including the 23rd, marched from Washington through Frederick, Maryland. There, where Barbara Fritchie supposedly defied Stonewall Jackson by defending the American flag, they were cheered like heroes. Fritchie reportedly gave the flag to General Jesse Reno, Hayes's corps commander. At South Mountain, Hayes and Reno got into a heated argument about foraging by Hayes's troops. Reno reportedly was on the brink of courtmartialing Hayes when the battle intervened. The 23rd was given the lead position of attack, Reno was killed, and Hayes was severely wounded.

I would prefer to be a good colonel, to a bad general.
    —On the reenlistment of the 23rd, October 10, 1863

In 1864 the 23rd was called to the Shenandoah Valley. There it fought under General David Hunter and ultimately under the dramatic General Phil Sheridan against Confederate General Jubal Early, who had invaded suburban Washington. During this period Hayes became essentially a brigadier general under a leader he greatly respected, General George Crook (of the Dayton, Ohio, area).

War is a cruel business, and there is brutality on all sides.
    —Letter to Lucy, July 2, 1864, about treatment of prisoners

The 23rd, the 36th Ohio, and two other regiments, with Hayes leading, played a key part in U.S. Army victories at Opequen and Fisher's Hill, Virginia. They were part of the United States defeat at Second Kernstown and the near defeat at Cedar Creek, Virginia, when Sheridan personally rallied the troops to victory. (Sheridan's ride became the subject of a dramatic poem by Thomas B. Read.) That victory finished the Confederate army in the Valley and contributed substantially to Lincoln's reelection victory in 1864. Hayes, who acted as a brigadier general in several battles, was ultimately given that title. He was elected to Congress in 1864 but refused to serve until the war was over.

Hayes left the war a genuine if quiet hero, a man of courage, intelligence, and compassion. He loved his troops and was beloved by them. Although he was elected to Congress twice, the Ohio governorship three times, and the Presidency, he never found any thing so vivid and stimulating as his life with the 23rd.

As we grow older, and our army stories grow larger, we thank God we are able to believe them.
—A typical Hayes quote to Civil War veterans in the late 1880's

~

Part III: Hayes in Politics

Politics is a bad trade...Guess we'll quit.
—Letter to Lucy, July 9, 1865

The great idea of the Nation, according to Mr. Lincoln... is expressed in the Declaration...'We hold these truths to be self-evident, that all men are created equal...' (The words) are simple, their meaning plain, and their truth undoubted...The equality declared by the fathers (was) an equality of rights. Foolish attempts have been made by those who hate the principles of the fathers to destroy the great fundamental truth of the Declaration by limiting the phrase 'all men' to the men of a single race...
—Speech at Lebanon, Ohio, August 5, 1867

Hayes, with a reddish cast to his hair and ruddy complexion, of average height and strong build, was in his way a handsome man. He was well-educated, sensible, sociable, and compassionate, a man of the people. He did not need political office to make his life meaningful, and most of the time he did not seek it. While in the front lines in the Civil War (he called it the War of Rebellion) he was nominated in 1864 for a seat in Congress from Hamilton County. He agreed to run with the proviso that he would not campaign nor would he serve until the fighting was ended. He was elected but did not serve until September of 1865. With its seniority system and often blowhard rhetoric, he did not like Congress and left after two years. Politically, Hayes was not very partisan. Important political ideas to him were that he thought all people should be educated, have reasonable opportunities, and be treated fairly.

In 1867 Hayes was approached by friends to run for Governor of Ohio. He agreed to run, ultimately three times, defeating three

Governor Hayes and daughter, Fanny, about 1870

prominent Democrats: Allen Thurman and William Allen of Chillicothe and "Gentleman George" Pendleton of Cincinnati. If one wonders why no Democrat from Ohio was ever elected President, a substantial reason was Hayes. All three of his gubernatorial opponents had national visibility and might have been nominated for President had they beaten Hayes. Hayes also beat an outstanding Republican for the nomination, Alfonso Taft, father of William Howard Taft, and grandfather of Robert A. Taft, "Mr. Republican" of the 1940s and 1950s.

The great task is to educate a whole people in...high virtues, to the end that they may be equal to their opportunities and dangers that surround them. The chief instrumentalities in this education are the home, the school, the platform, the pulpit, the press, and all good men and women...
    —Speech at Cincinnati, April 7, 1872

Hayes was a progressive governor, supporting universal suffrage for North and South, civil service and penal reform. He cut the state deficit, simplified government, and sought lower taxes at the local level. Reflecting his interests in science, education, and the practical arts, he commissioned the first geological survey of the state and was one of the founders of Ohio Agriculture and Mechanical College, later The Ohio State University.

The big issue of his last term was the payment of bonds in gold rather than "greenbacks." Hayes, a politician of conviction, thought this was the only honorable thing to do. This was a major national issue pitting lenders against debtors, with the Republicans generally supporting the former. This and its latter positions on high tariffs helped identify the Republicans with the well-to-do and big business.

Let me assure my country men of the Southern States that if I shall be charged with the duty of organizing an administration, it will be one which will regard and cherish their truest interests—the interests of white and colored people both, and equally; and which will put forth its best efforts in behalf of a civil policy which will wipe out forever the distinction between North and South in our common country.

—Letter of acceptance of nomination, July 8, 1876

Part IV: President

A. Election 1876

Hayes received the Republican nomination for President in 1876 because he was every one's second choice. His strategy was brilliant, either because he was indifferent or because his allies were extremely disciplined. The election of 1876 became the most disputed of any election in American history. Ironically, the two major candidates of 1876 were both reformers. Many historians say Samuel J. Tilden of New York won because he had the majority of popular votes, and lost the electoral college because of three disputed states in the South. However, there was murder and intimidation of mostly Republican black voters in the South, organized by white supremacists in violation of the Fourteenth and Fifteenth Amendments to the Constitution. At that time the Democratic party had often made racist appeals, and Hayes and others thought that a Democratic victory

DEMOCRATS

'PUT UP'

OR

SHUT UP

I Want to BET From

$100 to $500!

THAT R. B. HAYES

Will be elected President of the United States of America. The money is now deposited at the office of the HERALD AND UNION.

Nov. 6th, 1876.   **GEORGE MARLETTE.**

would partly negate the victory of the United States in the Civil War.

A little less than 16 years ago I marched down High Street with one thousand
men to pass to the East and South to do what we could to restore the Union of the States.
In that work we were eminently successful, so far as it was possible to be successful by the force
of arms... Of my comrades over one third and over never returned to their homes...
   —Farewell to the citizens of Ohio from Columbus,
March 1, 1877

Hayes's (and the nation's) first problem was to get the disputed election resolved. There was much temptation for chicanery and demagoguery. Despite this, Hayes showed himself to be cool and rational, acting with the fatalism he had demonstrated in the Civil War and in securing the Republican nomination. An electoral commission was appointed to examine the votes of three disputed states. Two days before inauguration it ruled in Hayes's favor. Some southerners threatened rebellion, but a compromise was worked out which Tilden supported. Hayes set forth a straightforward program for moderate reform, in human rights, currency, and civil service. He also committed himself to one term in office.

He serves his party best who serves his country best.
   —Inaugural Address, March 5, 1877

B. Presidency (1877-1881)

Hayes began his presidency by picking three outstanding men for his cabinet: William Evarts as Secretary of State, John Sherman (of Lancaster, Ohio) as Secretary of the Treasury and Carl Schurz as Secretary of Interior. Hayes did this without consulting party leaders, which immediately offended them. He also appointed an outstanding Supreme Court Justice, John Marshall Harlan. Politically, Hayes remained rather non-partisan. Serious issues for him were the value of currency, civil service reform, education, and equal rights. As President, Hayes was clever and patient, picking issues carefully and frequently winning partial victories under difficult circumstances. During his entire term, Democrats outnumbered Republicans in the House, and during the second half of his term, in the Senate.

During his term a major battle with Congress was the implementation of the Fourteenth and Fifteenth Amendments to the Constitution. Hayes sought to

Hayes's inauguration, March 5, 1877: "He serves his party best who serves his country best."

strengthen voter rights. Congress would not appropriate money for enforcement, or would try to abolish civil rights and other laws by putting riders on appropriations bills. Hayes vetoed the bills and ultimately made his point.

At the White House the Hayeses had a major impact. They brought their five children (ages 6-24) who created a cheerful, rambunctious atmosphere. Lucy started the tradition of the Easter egg roll and alcohol was banned. Secretary of State William Evarts, a clever man, said of one official White House dinner, "It was a brilliant affair; the water flowed like champagne."

Hayes was the classical reasonable man surrounded by unreasonable conditions and people. In the South, Lincoln's policy of conciliation had never been followed. After Lincoln's death there was much hatred. Some southern leaders reacted viciously to those citizens least able to protect themselves, the blacks. The 14th and 15th amendments, designed to protect ex-slaves, were not enforced where white supremacists ruled.

Hayes understood the wisdom of Lincoln's policies. Hayes thought education was the solution to most of the nation's problems. With education at all levels Hayes thought the South would become more like the North, adapting to the new commercial society of the late nineteenth century. Unfortunately, it took another century for that to happen. With education, ex-slaves could be productive and free, advancing economically just as many immigrants had done. So, too, could poor whites. The well-to-do could easily adjust to the commercial world. They needed to renew their sense of justice, of *noblesse oblige*, and to enforce the 14th and 15th Amendments. This would advance the entire country and, coincidentally, the fortunes of progressive Republicans.

The southern policy of Hayes, like that of Lincoln, generally failed. Almost a century of hatred and bitterness followed. It was a loss for everyone. Hayes deserves credit for seeing the problem and trying to do something about it, just as we honor Jefferson for his phrase "...all men are created equal...", and Lincoln for his cogent arguments against slavery.

Hayes's second big issue was Civil Service reform. Since Andrew Jackson, the winning political parties had often run the government in a partisan political manner at great cost to the country. Presidents generally deferred to Congressmen or Senators for Federal appointments. The Civil Service was often incompetent or corrupt. The scandals during the period of the Grant administration were the greatest the country had seen, deeply embarrassing to reform Republicans. The party split in 1872, partly on this issue. As President, Hayes quietly sided with the reformers, which offended party regulars who depended on the Civil Service for manpower and political contributions.

If there are any two men in the country whose opposition and hatred are a certificate of good character, they are Conkling and Butler. I enjoy the satisfaction of being fully endorsed by the hatred and opposition of both these men.
—Diary, January 16, 1881

Hayes took on Conkling, and Chester Alan Arthur of The New York Customs House. Hayes played his hand cautiously and cleverly. In the end, he won a few modest reforms, including getting rid of Arthur. Ironically, Arthur later as President became one of the country's greatest Civil Service reformers.

Like many Republicans, Hayes was a hard money man. For him the issue was simple. He thought it morally right that the value of the currency be stable. This was manifested in his policies on gold, silver, and greenbacks. The policies were generally supported by the lenders and attacked by the debtors, many of whom were farmers. Hayes, at the time land rich but cash poor, essentially acted against his own personal interests, an approach not widely followed by many political leaders. The value of the currency, *e.g.*, inflation, deflation, interest rates, has always been an American political issue, and it remains so today.

The Indians are certainly entitled to our sympathy and a conscientious respect on our part for their claims upon our sense of justice...Many, if not most, of our Indian wars have had their origin in broken promises and acts of injustice on our part...We can not expect them to improve, and to follow our guidance unless we keep faith with them in respecting the rights they possess...The faithful performance of our promises is the first condition of a good nderstanding...I can not too urgently recommend to Congress that prompt and liberal provision be made for the conscientious fulfillment be made of all engagements entered into by Government and the Indian people.

—Message to Congress, December 3, 1877

Early in the Hayes administration there were serious mistakes in regards to members of the Ponca and Nez Perce tribes. Hayes's general policies towards Indians was to educate them and to integrate them into American society. His ideas were progressive and he was apologetic when they did not always work out.

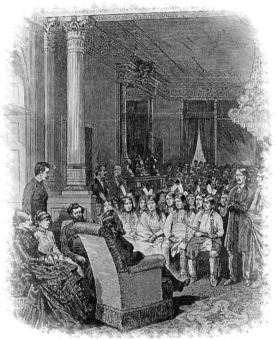

As the Chief Executive at the time when the wrong was consummated, I am deeply sensible that enough of the responsibility for that wrong justly attaches to me to make it

Engraving of Hayes entitled "Pow-pow at White House"

my particular duty and earnest desire to do all I can to give the injured people that measure of redress which is required by justice and humanity...

—Message to Congress, February 1, 1881

In 1877 there was a major labor strike. This was an outgrowth of the depression of 1873 and attempts of railroad management to roll back wages. Management wanted the army to intervene against the strikers. The strike was tragic with loss of life in Pittsburgh, Baltimore, and other railroad centers. Hayes protected Federal property, but did not directly intervene in the strike. Ultimately the strike was settled by the appropriate parties. (In Indianapolis, Benjamin

Harrison, lawyer and future President, mediated between the workers and railroad management.) After he left the presidency Hayes criticized the "plutocrats," rich and selfish men operating against the public interest.

~

Part V: After the Presidency

It may be truly said that for twenty five years, at least, railroad working men have had too little, and railroad capitalists, those that have controlled and manipulated the railroads, have had too much...The public has been neglected; its rights and interests disregarded. The railroads should be under a wise, watchful, and powerful supervision of Government.
     —Diary, May 2, 1886

When his term was up, Hayes was pleased to leave the presidency. He and Lucy returned home to Fremont, Ohio, to lead an active social life and to work involving education. Hayes served on the Slater fund and the Peabody fund, which gave money and support for education for poor and minorities, and on the board of Ohio State. One of the most famous students who got a grant because of Hayes was William E. B. Dubois who became the country's pre-eminent black intellectual.

Lucy, one of the most popular first ladies ever, was sought by many organizations. Francis Willard sought her for involvement in temperance matters and Susan B. Anthony for involvement in the woman's suffrage movement. But Lucy was more of a nurturer than an advocate. She became involved in the Methodist Home Missionary Society. Its purpose, in those pre-welfare days, was to help the poor, primarily women and children.

The lifting of the lowly of our country ought to interest every man and woman.
     —Lucy W. Hayes, October 28, 1886

In retirement the Hayeses were much honored and beloved. One of Hayes's biographers, Ari Hoogenboom, compared Hayes in his honesty, simplicity, and decency to the founders of the early American Republic, yet with his organization of reform, a forerunner to the political reformers of the twentieth century.

Hayes with grandson, Sherman Otis Hayes

●Deaths: Lucy Webb Hayes died of a stroke June 25, 1889, at age 58 at their home in Fremont.

Well, let the end come. The charm of life has left me, when Lucy died.
    —Diary, August 24, 1890

Although Hayes was a man's man, he was always dependent on one woman. First his sister, then his wife; after her death he became dependent on nieces and daughter. He was to continue an active life for more than three and a half years. He died at age 70 of a heart attack at his home, January 17, 1893.

He was a patriotic citizen, a lover of the flag and our free institutions, an industrious and conscientious civil officer, a soldier of dauntless courage, a loyal comrade and friend, a sympathetic and helpful neighbor, and the honored head of a happy Christian home. He has steadily grown in the public esteem, and the impartial historian will not fail to recognize the conscientiousness, the manliness, and courage that so strongly characterized his whole public career.
    —Eulogy by President Benjamin Harrison, January 20, 1893

●Visiting the Hayes's Sites

If one can know Grant best by his writings, especially his *Memoirs*, one can know the Hayeses best by visiting the home, museum, and library in Fremont, Ohio. The home is gracious, inviting, and comfortable, with an outlook upon the world. The library is the first Presidential library. Hayes's birthplace in Delaware, Ohio, was torn down in 1928. South Mountain in Maryland, where Hayes was severely wounded, is at a rest stop off I-70 near Boonsboro, Maryland. It is near the Civil War battlefield of Antietam.

●Works Relevant to Understanding the Hayeses

A. Biographical

●◆Barnard, Harry. 1967. *Rutherford B. Hayes and His America*. Indianapolis: Bobbs-Merrill Company, Inc.

➸Davison, Kenneth E. 1972. *The Presidency of Rutherford B. Hayes.* Westport, CT: Greenwood Press, Inc.

This book contains a series of short essays, putting Hayes into context. In one way the period of 1877–1881 was a great period of inventiveness, development, prosperity, and conciliation. Hayes deserves some credit for his outstanding appointments, honesty, and his sensible policies.

➸Eckenrode, H. J. 1930. *Rutherford B. Hayes: Statesman of Reunion.* New York: Dodd, Mead and Co.

➸Geer, Emily Apt. 1984. *First Lady, the Life of Lucy W. Hayes.* Kent State University Press, Kent, OH and the Rutherford B. Hayes Presidential Center, Fremont, OH.

Lucy was the perfect nineteenth century political wife, a natural nurturer of people, plants, and animals. She was intelligent and animated, with a gift of putting people at ease. On certain political issues she may have had stronger views than her husband, but she deferred to him in public. This book tells her story and of those around her that she nurtured.

➸Hoogenboom, Ari. 1988. *The Presidency of Rutherford B. Hayes.* Lawrence, KS: University Press of Kansas.

This is one of a series of contemporary books on presidents, well done, scholarly, and fair.

-1995. *Rutherford B. Hayes, Warrior and President.* Lawrence, KS: University Press of Kansas.

This is the most current, thorough and comprehensive biography of Hayes.

➸Williams, T. Harry. 1965. *Hayes of the Twenty-third.* New York: Arnold A. Knopf.

This is a fair and dramatic account of Hayes's Civil War years by the author of *Lincoln and His Generals,* and many other books.

B. Non-Biographical

1. On War

●**Remarque, Erich Maria.** 1928 (German- 1929 English). *All Quiet on the Western Front.* Boston, MA: Little Brown and Co.

●**Tuchman, Barbara W.** 1962. *The Guns of August.* New York: Macmillian and Co.
These books illustrate well Robert E. Lee's quote: "It is well that war is so terrible, or we should get too fond of it."

●**Shakespeare, William.** 1600 (est). *Henry V.*
Henry is a modest, thoughtful, and noble battlefield leader of a small but disciplined English army before it defeats the much larger French army in the Battle of Agincourt in 1415.

2. U. S. Constitution

●*Amendments Thirteen,* 1865; *Fourteen,* 1868; *Fifteen,* 1870;
The Thirteenth amendment abolishes slavery, completing the task of Lincoln's Emancipation Proclamation. The Fourteenth Amendment contains several provisions, the most important of which was to try to guarantee civil rights for all citizens. The Fifteenth Amendment was even more explicit on the right to vote for minorities and ex-slaves. Hayes supported the Fourteenth and Fifteenth Amendments and proposed legislation to carry them out. Tragically for the country, such legislation was not passed and enforced until the 1960's.

3. On Life

●**Bunyan, John.** 1678. *The Pilgrims Progress.* Widely available in paperback.
This book, of great influence in England and America, was Hayes's mother's favorite book. It is a dramatic and expressive work, showing vividly the English Puritan world-view.

●**Hawthorne, Nathaniel.** 1851. *The House of the Seven Gables.* Widely available in paperback.

The character of Phoebe, who brought light to a gloomy house, reminded Hayes of his wife Lucy.

●**Howells, William Dean.** 1885. *The Rise of Silas Lapham.* Widely available in paperback.

Howells, born in Martin's Ferry, Ohio, lived in Hamilton, Dayton, Ashtabula, Jefferson, and Columbus. He became a major literary figure in America. He was a personal friend of Hayes. This book, with an ironic title, set in the 1870's, deals in a complex way with a businessman and his family, and another family with "old money." It is an interesting reflection on the times.

●**Melville, Herman.** 1891 *Billy Budd, Foretopman.* Usually available with short works of Melville in paperback.

This is a story of uncalculating good confronting evil. It is a classic written by one of America's greatest writers.

●**Santmeyer, Helen H.** 1982. *And the Ladies of the Club;* New York: G. P. Putnam's Sons.

This is about the families of two Civil War veterans, their friends and others set in a small Xenia-like town in Ohio from 1868–1932. It includes appearances by Hayes and McKinley and offers an often fascinating discussion of the politics and economics of the times and their impact on ordinary people.

3. Poetry
One reason many students used to love history (and rhetoric) was that they studied historic poetry. The poetry, while often not literally true, was dramatic and vivid, capturing the spirit and *emotions* of the times. The following three poems, which used to be in every schoolbook, will probably have to be found by a librarian or a bookseller.

●**Read, Thomas B.** 1865. *Sheridan's Ride.*
This poem tells the story of Sheridan's dramatic ride and triumph at Cedar Creek.

●**Tennyson, Alfred Lord.** 1883 *In Memorium.*
This is a long work read by Hayes after Lucy's death.

●**Whittier, John Greenlief.** 1863. *Barbara Fritchie.*

This tells the story of an elderly lady of Frederick, Maryland, protecting the American flag against the troopers of Stonewall Jackson. Fritchie reportedly gave the flag to General Reno, who got in a heated argument with Hayes before the Battle of South Mountain, where Reno was killed and Hayes wounded.

James Abram Garfield

Promise destroyed

20th President
March 4, 1881–September 19, 1881

Garfield, the ambiguous. Born in a log cabin, a physically powerful but often clumsy canal worker, a charismatic idealistic preacher who charmed women more than he should have, husband of a bright and talented woman with her own ideas on national issues. He was a hero in the Civil War but not unequivocally. He was a student of everything yet also a teacher and education leader, a practical idealist, and emotional rationalist. People liked Garfield. Politics was natural to him. Did he use his political career to further his own fortune? Was he involved with the *Crédit Mobilier* scandal? As President, would he use his enormous talents and energy for the good of the country? Or was he a person without a center who would bend to the strongest wind? Garfield the ambiguous.

I am distressed by the curious state of conflict in my own mind upon the various phases of it. To be an extreme man is doubtless comfortable. It is painful to see too many sides of a subject.

—Journal 1878, Garfield on the tariff question

◀ *Garfield with daughter, Molly: a cheerful Ohio family in the White House.*

●**Family Heritage:** Garfield was born November 19, 1831, in a log cabin at Orange, Ohio, in Cuyahoga County, the youngest of four surviving children of Abram and Eliza Ballou Garfield. The first American immigrant Garfield left Chester, England, for Massachusetts in 1630. He lived in Watertown, Massachusetts. The later Garfields moved to Cooperstown, New York. James's father, Abram, was born in Worcester, New York. The Garfield men were famous for their feats of strength. Abram Garfield was a champion wrestler and a canal construction worker. He got sick, possibly with lung damage, after fighting a forest fire and died when James was 18 months old. Garfield's mother, Eliza Ballou, was of French Huguenot descent. Her ancestors settled in Providence, Rhode Island. She was born at Richmond, New Hampshire. When she was young, her family moved to Muskingum County in central Ohio. There she met Abram Garfield. They married and moved to the Western Reserve section in northern Ohio. Abram Garfield's death at a young age left the family impoverished, but Eliza's determination and some help from her relatives, the Boyntons, kept the family together. Eliza Ballou Garfield was religious but also joyful and musical. The Garfields were friendly and openly affectionate, a family of huggers.

●**Religion:** The Garfields were members of the Disciples of Christ (Christian) church, sometimes called Campbellites, after their leader Alexander Campbell. The Disciples believed in unifying all Christians through the return to early principles. James A. was converted to a life of lay preaching at age 19. This and his emotional rationality helped him develop his remarkable speaking abilities. Although Garfield developed many intellectual and cultural interests beyond religion, he stayed involved with the Disciples all of his life.

The longer I live, the firmer is my determination to obtain a thorough classical education. There is the path by which young men and young ladies can rise above the groveling herd.
    —Letter to Mary Hubbell, May 29, 1852

The ideal college is Mark Hopkins at one end of a log, and a student at the other end.
    —This is probably a paraphrase from a speech by Garfield, December 28, 1871. It states Garfield's fundamentalist view of the importance of the teacher as the key to education.

●**Education:** Garfield attended a variety of small and primitive schools in

Garfield grew up poor and thought poverty taught few lessons.

Orange, Chester, Solon, and Hiram, Ohio. He paid for his schooling by working as a janitor, woodcutter, and carpenter. Garfield was a driven, versatile, compulsive learner. He entered Western Reserve Eclectic Institute (later Hiram College) as a student and left as a teacher. He entered Williams College in Williamstown, Massachusetts, as a junior and became a noted local speaker. At Williams, Garfield had the great teacher, Mark Hopkins. Hopkins, a genial man, sought to reconcile science and religion, encouraging students to think for themselves. Garfield was a lifelong learner of great zeal. His initial interests were religion and philosophy, Latin, Greek, classical history and culture, science, mathematics, and literature.

●**Wife:** After a long and somewhat wavering courtship, James married Lucretia Rudolph, November 11, 1858. Lucretia (Crete) was the nice-looking daughter of Zebulon Rudolph, a Disciple, farmer, and a founder of The Eclectic Institute. Crete was a calm, intelligent, dignified, scholarly woman who taught school before marrying Garfield. They shared a love of great literature: Shakespeare, Goethe, Dickens, Jane Austen. Throughout their lives, both Crete and James were often

sick. They were parents of four sons and one daughter who lived to maturity. One son and one daughter died as infants.

I have been wonderfully blessed in the discretion of my wife. She is one of the coolest and best balanced women I ever saw. She is unstampedeable. There has not been one solitary instance of my public career when I suffered in the smallest degree for any remark she ever made...
  —James A Garfield

After all that I hear, there seems to be something within me, I cannot name it, that whispers fearful words into my heart. It tells me that I'm not honest—that all of this is a pretense on my part—that there is no such thing as human sincerity or honesty.
  —*Journal of Daily Events and Private Cogitations: or his Confidential Friend to Whom he entrusts the Secret Thoughts of His Heart*, April 10, 1853, after breaking up with Mary Hubbell.

Lucretia Garfield and her husband shared an intellectual life.

To some men the fact that they came from poverty...is a matter of pride...I lament sorely I was born to poverty...Let no man praise me because I was born poor...It was very bad for my life.
  —Letter to J. H. Rhodes, November 19, 1862

There is a spirit in me that can rise up to the level of the occasion when it comes—and yet more—can ride the waves and balance itself upon the rocky elements. Napoleon felt it as he was going over the bridge at Lodi, that he had the power to lead, and I have had it told to me by my inner consciousness.
  —Journal, October 3, 1857

●**Personal Characteristics:** Garfield was a complex man. He was sensitive and self-conscious about being poor. He was intuitive. He was a lifetime learner from books and people, a voracious reader in all fields. He had the capability of seeing all sides of an issue. This and his agreeable and jovial personality led many people to think that he agreed with them. Later, when it turned out that he didn't, they accused him of deception. He was impressive physically, handsome in his own way, big and strong, with a large head and riveting light blue eyes. He was tactile and passionate. He liked women and they liked him. At school he liked his students, in the army he liked the troops of the 42nd Ohio, and he loved his country. He communicated this well, and people liked him for it. He enjoyed being liked and was accused of being too accommodating. Despite his intellectual background he made his strongest commitments on an emotional basis. At age 19 he was moved sufficiently by an evangelist to become a lay minister. He had a luke-warm commitment against slavery until he encountered ragged and forlorn slaves in the Civil War. From that he made a lifetime commitment to their freedom and education. Garfield was a gifted speaker with a strong voice, a magnetic presence who spoke and wrote clearly. Garfield was also frequently sick, some of it probably psychosomatic, which was likely his way of dealing with stress. Garfield was also honest and introspective enough to recognize his own failings and to continuously work on them.

The sin of slavery is one of which it may be that without the shedding of blood there is no remission.
   —Letter to Burke Hinsdale, January 5, 1861

Gen. McClellan is weakly and wickedly conservative...and the President nearly as bad. But out of the very weakness and timidity of our leaders, I draw the hope that thus God has willed it—that he is the commander-in-chief of our armies, and there is no thwarting of Divine purpose. If McClellan will discipline and mobilize the people into armies, and let them meet the enemy, God will take care of the grand consequences.
   —Letter to J. H. Rhodes, February 12, 1862

Part I: Garfield in the Civil War

Garfield entered the Civil War as a lieutenant colonel of volunteers. Like Hayes, he learned military strategy and tactics from books as well as by talking to professional soldiers. Early in the war he was given a brigade and orders to attack in the Sandy Valley in southeast Kentucky. He freed the area from rebel armies and although this was not a major battle Garfield became a hero in Ohio and promoted to brigadier general.

After being reassigned to a West Point general whom Garfield did not like, Garfield headed for Shiloh. He arrived after the battle and was shocked by the massive carnage on each side. Later he was assigned to the boring duty of guarding bridges and railroads. He didn't like the duty and became sick. In 1862 he was elected to Congress from the district encompassing Ashtabula, Trumbull, Mahoning, Geauga, and Portage Counties. He became a good friend of Secretary of Treasury Salmon P. Chase (of Worthington and Cincinnati, Ohio) and an acquaintance of Secretary of War, Edwin Stanton. In late 1863 Garfield was assigned as a military juror in the court martial of General Fitz-John Porter, the Army's designated scapegoat for the loss of the second battle of Bull Run. Under General David Hunter, Garfield and eight other officers found Porter guilty, a miscarriage of justice. The case was difficult for Garfield. He had his Army ambitions, but he must have seen Porter's side of the case. At the end of the case Garfield was eager to get out of Washington.

On January 25, 1863, with a letter of introduction signed by Secretary Chase, Garfield was assigned to hyperactive General William Rosecrans (from Delaware County, Ohio), the original commander of the 23rd Ohio. Rosecrans, who had replaced General Don Carlos Buell was a leader of great energy and commanded the Army of the Cumberland to a difficult victory near Murfreesboro, Tennessee (Stones River). Rosecrans was initially wary of Garfield, a preacher and politician turned soldier. He met with him for three weeks before offering him an assignment. He found Garfield bright, a good writer, knowledgeable about many things. Moreover, he was the one person in camp that seemed to match Rosecrans in interests and energy. Rosecrans offered Garfield the position of chief of staff, and came to rely greatly on Garfield for advice.

In June of 1863 Rosecrans outmaneuvered Confederate General Braxton Bragg, forcing him to withdraw south of the Tennessee River. Garfield suggested the

For his heroic actions at Chickamauga, Garfield was promoted to major general. ▶

76

removal of two ineffective generals, Alexander McCook and Thomas Crittenden, but Rosecrans, to his great detriment, rejected Garfield's advice. Garfield wanted him to attack, but Rosecrans (like McClellan an engineering officer) was slow, wanting more cavalry and supplies from Washington. Garfield wrote a letter to Secretary Chase expressing his frustration with Rosecrans. Chase showed his letter to Secretary of War Stanton, which undercut Rosecrans's request for more cavalry and supplies.

> *I have restrained hitherto, lest I do injustice to a good man, and say things which better left unsaid....I cannot conceal from you the fact that I have been greatly dissatisfied with the slow progress...since Stone River...(and) could not feel but there was not that live and earnest determination to fling the great weight of this army into the scale and make its power felt in crushing the Rebellion....*
> —Letter to Secretary Chase, July 27, 1863

In September of 1863 Rosecrans allowed his army to be spread out, and the Confederates attacked at Chickamauga. It was a devastating two-day battle in which Garfield played a dangerous and somewhat heroic role, carrying communications between generals. The U. S. Army eventually retreated and regrouped. McCook and Crittenden did not do well, but General George Thomas, who held the line (with troops mostly from the Midwest) when all around retreated, became "The Rock of Chickamauga" and successor to Rosecrans. Garfield was promoted to major general after the battle.

Garfield's part in Rosecrans's downfall illustrates the difference between his character and that of Rosecrans, Grant, and Hayes. Rosecrans refused to remove two sub-standard generals, which likely contributed to the disaster at Chickamauga, which contributed to his removal as an important commander. Grant, a quiet man, tried to advance the meritorious and get rid of the incompetent. He was stuck with many political generals, among the worst being Banks and Butler. They were both politically influential. Despite all his prestige he felt he had to wait until they were publicly humiliated before he could remove them. This happened and he did. Hayes was more straightforward. He was an honorable man, satisfied mainly being a colonel of the 23rd Ohio. If he didn't like what someone did, he confronted them or said nothing. Garfield, a staff man to Rosecrans, gave his honest opinion on McCook and Crittenden and he was probably right. Rosecrans was Garfield's friend and sponsor; he listened to Garfield and often accepted his advice. The most important thing to Garfield, however, was to win the war. It was undoubtedly with great pain that he took the initiative to give his honest opinion about Rosecrans's leadership. This ended their friendship and caused many to consider Garfield as treacherous. Garfield had to be satisfied that he served the greater cause.

~

Part II: Congress 1863-1880

When Garfield met with Lincoln, he asked him where he thought he could best serve. Lincoln, who already had many political generals and was clever about people, advised him to serve in Congress, where his first-hand knowledge of the war could be used to help the Army. This ended Garfield's Army career. He was assigned to a military committee under Robert Schenck (an expert poker player from Franklin, Ohio). Unlike Hayes, Garfield enjoyed Congress. He considered himself a well-educated, practical man who could get things done.

One should remember that Garfield was 32 when he became active in Congress. By force of personality, his vivid speaking ability, and hard work, he quickly became a leader. Initially, Garfield sided with the Radical Republicans. Lincoln, characterized by Garfield as a second-rate lawyer from Illinois, meant well but was too cautious and slow. Prior to Lincoln's death, it is likely Garfield would have joined the hard-liners in asserting congressional prerogatives against the executive branch. Lincoln, a masterful politician who was continuously underrated, might have had an opportunity to end the war and reconcile the nation.

When Lincoln died and Andrew Johnson became President, everything changed. Johnson's obstreperous personality made it easy to vote against his policies. He hoped for a quick reconciliation, but this was unacceptable to the southern hard-liners and the Radical Republicans in Congress. Garfield voted for one of the great overreaches in American history by Congress: the Tenure of Office Act. This law prohibited the President from removing certain executive branch officials. When Johnson defied Congress it voted to impeach him for violation of that act.

Garfield thought the South had a feudal system and the abolition of slavery removed support for the system, without removing the system. He thought the Federal Government must be coercive to change the system to create a system of free labor. This was different from Hayes's views, which were more conciliatory and optimistic. For a long term solution, their views were similar, both believing that education provided the answer for whites and blacks. Garfield supported the founding of Hampton Institute for blacks, and Gallaudet College for the deaf, and wrote and sponsored a bill for a sub-cabinet Department of Education.

Garfield, who was elected to Congress nine times, became an important legislator with a particular interest in financial matters. After his experience on the Military Affairs Committee he became a member of the Ways and Means Committee and later the chairman of the House Appropriations Committee, where he mastered many of the details of Federal expenditures. His views were anti-inflationary, supporting Federal payments in gold, rather than paper currency.

I believe that any party which commits itself to paper money will go down amid the general disaster, covered with the curses of a ruined people.
—Letter to B. A. Hinsdale, December 15, 1867

On the other big party issue of the day, the tariff, he tried to find a middle ground. His view was that the tariff should be moderately reformed or that some day it would be drastically cut with severe consequences. Like many of his views, this was sophisticated and far-seeing.

In regard to the Republican party, he generally steered an independent course between the two main Republican factions, the Stalwarts under Roscoe Conkling, boss of New York, and the half-breeds under James G. Blaine. The difference between the two factions was more about personalities and political jobs than ideology, although the Stalwarts were anti-civil service.

Your decision will mark an era in American history. The just and final settlement of this great question will take a high place among the achievements of this decade. It will establish forever this truth, of inestimable value to us and to mankind, that a republic can wield the vast enginery of war without breaking down the safeguards of liberty; can suppress insurrection, and put down rebellion, however formidable, without destroying the bulwarks of law.
—Argument before Supreme Court in *ex parte Milligan,*
March 6, 1866

Garfield practiced some law as a Congressman. He was criticized for his legal involvement in the awarding of pavement contracts to the DeGolyer Company of Chicago, while head of the House Appropriations Committee. He was also im-

Garfield was a Radical Republican who became an artful politician. ▶

plicated in a minor way in the *Crédit Mobilier* financial affair. The truth remains unclear, but no charges were ever proven against him. His outstanding legal case was *ex parte Milligan* where he successfully argued before the Supreme Court against a military court's jurisdiction over civilians where civil courts were operating. It stands today as one of our great civil rights cases.

~
Part III: Election as President, 1880

As promised, Hayes declined to run for a second term. Most of the Republican leaders welcomed this since Hayes was more of a reformer than they wanted. The Stalwart Republicans under Roscoe Conkling wanted to bring back the good old days by nominating General Grant for a third term. The Half Breeds were pushing James G. Blaine, an imaginative, likable, energetic but tainted politician. Garfield was a potential candidate because of his Civil War record and his long service in Congress. He agreed, however, to support Hayes's Treasury Secretary and former senator from Ohio, John Sherman (brother of General William T. Sherman). The key to blocking Grant for the nomination was doing away with the unit voting rule, whereby all delegates from a state were forced to vote as a unit. Garfield supported the majority in doing away with the rule. Conkling made an impressive speech for Grant, and Garfield followed with an impressive speech for Sherman. Then the convention deadlocked for thirty-five ballots. Finally, led by reformers in Wisconsin and a future President, Benjamin Harrison, then of Indiana, Garfield was chosen. As a concession to the Stalwarts, Chester A. Arthur, the man Hayes fired as

FARMER GARFIELD
Cutting a Swath to the White House.

customs collector for New York, was chosen as Vice-President. Garfield won the election by about 40,000 votes over another former Civil War general and hero at Gettysburg, Winfield Scott Hancock, of Pennsylvania. The Greenback Labor (nominee James B. Weaver, born Dayton, Ohio) and Prohibition parties also ran candidates.

The elevation of the negro race from slavery to the full rights of citizenship is the most important change we have known since the adoption of the Constitution in 1787. No thoughtful man can fail to appreciate its beneficent effect upon our institutions and people.
—Inaugural Address, March 4, 1881

Part IV: Presidency

The Garfields moved into the White House with James's mother, Eliza, and a lively family of five children whose ages ranged from 8 to 18. The principal problem that Garfield wrestled with was Federal appointments. He offended the Stalwarts by appointing James G. Blaine as Secretary of State and by putting his own man, William H. Robertson, in as port collector of New York. It is unclear if this was clever or accidental strategy, but it caused Conkling and his close associate, "Me Too" Platt, to resign their Senate seats. They were not reappointed and Conkling was essentially finished as a political power. Garfield also ordered the new Postmaster General, Thomas L. James, to investigate fully the Star Route postal contract scandal, which went back to the Grant administration and implicated the secretary of the Republican National Committee, S. W. Dorsey, and his family. Garfield said, "Let the chips fall where they may." Critics of the Garfield administration thought Blaine (considered five times for the Republican nomination for President) would dominate the Garfield administration, which was possible. Blaine, despite his shady reputation, seemed to serve the country well in both the Garfield and Benjamin Harrison administrations.

I am greatly dissatisfied with my lack of opportunity for study. My day is frittered away with the personal seeking of people when it ought to be given to the problems which concern the whole country...some civil service reform will come by necessity after the wearisome years of wasted Presidents have paved the way for it.
—Journal, June 13, 1881

This engraving depicted the attack on Garfield's life at the railroad depot in July of 1881.

Garfield was stalked for a number of weeks by a crazed office seeker, Charles J. Guiteau. Guiteau had been inflamed by editorials from Stalwart newspapers who spoke of Garfield's treachery and betrayals. Guiteau bought a .44 pistol and systematically practiced shooting it at a canal near the White House. When rebuffed by Blaine for a job as counsel to Paris, he made up his mind. After sending to the White House a warning letter that was not seriously considered, Guiteau went to the Baltimore and Potomac railroad station to shoot Garfield. Garfield was sending off the sick Crete to Elberon, New Jersey, for rest and recovery and Guiteau, upon seeing the frail Crete, delayed his plans. On July 2, 1881, Garfield and Blaine returned to the station. Garfield was taking a long holiday to see Crete. This time Guiteau acted, and shot Garfield.

> *He must be insane. Why should he want to kill me?*
> —Garfield's comments about Guiteau, est. July 1881

The shots were not immediately fatal; one grazed his arm but the other went through his abdomen into his back. After returning to the White House, there were a number of doctors in attendance, some of whom probed for the bullet with unclean hands. They couldn't find it and called in Alexander Graham Bell to locate the bullet electrically. This, too, was unsuccessful. In the meanwhile Garfield generally remained conscious, dictating a letter to his mother in mid-August telling her that he was gaining every day. In early September he started to decline. He became afflicted with septicemia (blood poisoning) that led to pneumonia. He was transferred by train to Elberon, New Jersey, where he died on September 19, 1881.

Garfield, who served about four months prior to being shot, is not generally ranked by historians. The following President and former political hack, Chester Alan Arthur, is instead ranked as a good President, an example of how the office can inspire the man to rise to the occasion. If the learned, passionate, adaptable Garfield had lived, perhaps he would have been a great President. Perhaps some of the economic or social problems of the country that continued into the twentieth century would have not as been as severe. Based upon his pre-Presidential record, and his luck or skill in getting rid of Conkling, Garfield would likely have been—at least—a good president with substantive accomplishments.

Gently, silently, the love of a great people bore the pale sufferer to the longed-for-healing by the sea, to live or die, as God should will, within sight of its heaving bellows, within sound of its manifold voices. With wan, fevered face lifted to the cooling breeze, he looked out wistfully on the ocean's changing wonders, - on its far sails, whitening in the morning light; on its restless waves, rolling shoreward to break and die beneath the noonday sun; on the red clouds of evening, arching low in the horizon; on the serene and shining pathway of the stars. Let us think that his dying eyes read a mystic meaning which only a rapt and parting soul may know. Let us believe that in the silence of the receding world he heard the great waves breaking on a further shore, and felt already on his wasted brow the breath of the eternal morning.
—James G. Blaine's tribute to Garfield, February 27, 1882

●**Deaths:** Garfield died by the sea, in Elberon, New Jersey, on September 19, 1881. His mother, Eliza Ballou Garfield, died in 1888. Lucretia Rudolph Garfield organized Garfield's papers. She remained interested in politics the rest of her life, supporting Woodrow Wilson in the 1912 election. She died March 14, 1914.

Garfield's home in Mentor, Ohio.

●Visiting Garfield Sites

The Garfield house, formerly on farmland, is off I-90 on state route 615, northeast of Cleveland. James and Crete are buried in Lakeview Cemetery on U. S. 322, Mayfield Road, near Euclid Avenue in Cleveland.

●Works Relevant to Understanding the Garfields

A. Biographical

➪Caldwell, Robert G. 1931. *James A. Garfield, Party Chieftain.* New York: Dodd, Mead and Co.
A good short work on Garfield.

➪Leech, Margaret; Brown, Harry J. 1978. *The Garfield Orbit: The Life of President James A. Garfield.* New York: Harper and Row.

This book was started by the Pulitzer Prize winning author of *Reveille in Washington,* but unfortunately she died before finishing it. The book is still readable and good.

Muzzey, David Saville. 1934. *James G. Blaine, A Political Idol of Other Days.* New York: Dodd, Mead and Co.

Bright, personable, and articulate, Blaine was a major force in the Republican party from 1860-1893 and was seriously considered for the Republican nomination as President five times. He probably had more to do with blocking Grant's third term than anybody. He was also Secretary of State under (and accused of dominating) both Garfield and Harrison. Unfortunately he suffered the reputation of taking ethical or moral shortcuts in his public life. Muzzey was a first class historian and the book is very fair.

Peskin, Allan G. 1978. *Garfield.* Kent OH: Kent State University Press.

This is the dramatic Garfield with all his contradictory features, a good, objective, well-documented book (although I believe it misstates the character of Hayes, who served out of a sense of duty rather than ambition.

Taylor, John M. 1970. *Garfield of Ohio: The Available Man.* New York: W. W. Norton and Company.

B. Non-Biographical

Austen, Jane. Written 1796, first published 1813. *Pride and Prejudice:* widely available in paperback.

Jane Austen was an author that was beloved by the Garfields. This is a very clever book about English society, and finding suitable matches for a family of daughters.

Dreiser, Theodore. 1914. *The Titan.* New York: A Signet Classic, New American Library.

This is the second of two books in a trilogy by Dreiser. It shows in great detail the entangled corruption of business and government in the nineteenth century.

Eliot, George (Mary Ann Evans). 1861. *Silas Marner:* widely available in paperback.

This is a book that was likely read and discussed by the Grants, the Hayes, and the Garfields. Set in a small English village, it is about class, materialism, and family values.

●**Shakespeare, William.** *Hamlet.* 1602

Hamlet was forced into a role he did not want because of his father's murder. He equivocated. Garfield was by nature a scholar who could see all sides to an issue. He also liked people and liked to be liked. These characteristics gave him the appearance of lacking conviction, of being indecisive. This caused him problems all his life.

●**Sweet, William Warren.** 1950. *The Story of Religion in America.* New York: Harper and Bothers.

Religion had a great impact on Garfield and his family. They were immediately influenced by Alexander Campbell and the Disciples of Christ (later merged with the Christian Church founded by Barton Stone). Campbell and his father Thomas were well-educated Scots-Irish Presbyterians who revolted against creeds, church government, all the sects, and "man-made" additions to religion and wanted to return to the simplicity of the early church. Alexander Campbell was a gifted speaker, debater, and writer (at times comparable to Thomas Paine or Voltaire). The church had lay ministers who could learn the few simple essentials of their beliefs. Garfield was one of their lay ministers, developing his superb speaking style through preaching. Ironically, the reform that fought against sectarianism became another sect. Sweet puts the Campbellite and other reforms of religion in America in context in a very fair and objective way, relating it well to the history of the country.

●**Twain, Mark and Warner, Charles Dudley.** 1873. *The Gilded Age.* available in paperback.

This is the book that gave its name to its age. It's about money, work, ambition, and although satirical, it gives an interesting picture of the times. It includes a cynical picture of Washington and creates one unforgettable character in Colonel Eschol (later Beriah) Sellers, modeled on an uncle of Twain's. The book has its seams and one can guess what Twain wrote and what Warner wrote.

Benjamin Harrison
Hoosier from Ohio

23rd President
March 4, 1889-March 4, 1893

He had the famous name but it wasn't enough. He became a zealous Presbyterian, grimly throwing himself into his work. While still young he became a good lawyer. When the Civil War came he joined the cause and fervently supported it. Like Hayes, he was an excellent battlefield leader with unstoppable courage. When it was over he returned successfully to the law. He and his artistic wife were drawn into politics where, almost accidentally, he became President. He approached the Presidency as a lawyer, essentially becoming the country's national counsel. But he remained grim, serious, and humorless. He was a good President whom no one liked.

I want it understood I am the grandson of nobody. I believe every man should stand on his own merits.

—From campaign speech for John C. Fremont, first Republican candidate for President, est. September, 1856

◀ *Benjamin Harrison: He was an inherently methodical man, a legal expert with a focus on detail.*

●Family Heritage: Harrison was born August 20, 1833, at North Bend, Ohio. His father was John Scott Harrison, middle child of William Henry and Anna Symmes Harrison, reputedly his parents' favorite. It was a tragic family, with only two of the ten children living beyond the age of 40. John Scott Harrison was widowed twice. By his first wife, Lucretia Johnson Harrison, he had two daughters; by his second wife, Elizabeth (Ramsey) Irwin, four sons including Benjamin and two daughters. Elizabeth Irwin was from a family of Scottish Presbyterians in Mercersburg, Pennsylvania. Although the family was serious about religion, Elizabeth was musical and had a joyful personality. She died in 1850, immediately before Benjamin's 17th birthday. Benjamin's father lived to be 74. He was a never-too-prosperous farmer who became a two-term Whig Congressman, opposed to the extension of slavery but worried that the abolitionists would bring turmoil to the country. The family supported each other in a remarkable way. John's letters to Benjamin show him to be compassionate, sensible, and wise. Benjamin's siblings' letters to him show that they were supportive and often humorous.

●Religion: Benjamin Harrison was serious about his Presbyterian beliefs. Presbyterianism was very strong in southern Ohio in the 1800's with the Beechers (including Harriet Beecher Stowe), John Rankin, and other Presbyterian leaders of the underground railroad. His religion gave Benjamin Harrison strong views on fundamental things: religion, country, work, and family. From his youth Harrison was serious and consistent.

Education is getting possession of your mind, so you can use facts as a good mechanic uses tools.
—Robert Hamilton Bishop, Harrison's most influential teacher

The manner by which women are treated is a good criterion to judge of the true state of society. If we know but this one feature in character of a nation, we may easily judge the rest. For as society advances, the true character of woman is discovered...and appreciated.
—From an essay by Benjamin Harrison at age 16

●Education: The Harrison children were raised on a farm where they were expected to do their chores. Benjamin, a middle child, pursued outdoor activities like hunting and fishing and seemed to learn much from his siblings, parents, and grandparents. Initially the children had tutors, and Ben was recognized as a bright child. At age 14 he attended Farmers College at Walnut Hills where he encountered Dr. Robert Hamilton Bishop, a demanding but enthusiastic and sympathetic teacher from Scotland. Bishop had been a professor of history and political economy at Transylvania College in Lexington, Kentucky, and the president of Miami University in Oxford, Ohio (called Yale of the West). His demand for facts and logic, not fancy rhetoric, influenced Harrison's writing and speaking style. Ben entered Miami University as a junior in 1850. He was a serious student, rec-

Ben Harrison's first wife, Caroline

ognized for his speaking ability. He graduated third in his class.

●**Wife:** Ben fell in love at age 15 or so with Caroline Lavinia Scott (Carrie), daughter of a Presbyterian minister and a chemistry professor at Farmers College, who later founded Oxford Female Institute at Oxford, Ohio. She was musical, artistic, and full of life, appealing greatly to the pious and often stoic Harrison. They were married in 1853 when he was 20 and she was 21. Of their several children they had a son and a daughter that survived. Carrie and the children brought out a human side of Harrison that the public never saw.

...I do the same thing every day...eat three meals...sleep six hours, and read dusty old law books the rest of the time.
　　　　—Letter to sister, Anna, March 31, 1853

None but knaves should ever enter the political arena.
—John Scott Harrison to Benjamin Harrison, February 2, 1854

●**Professions:** At Miami Harrison had a difficult time deciding whether he would become a minister or a lawyer. He opted for the latter, reading law under Bellamy Storer of the law firm Storer and Gwynne in Cincinnati. Harrison's workaholic ways and intelligence impressed both partners. He did not like the city, however, with its dirt, pollution, and noise. After his marriage he moved to Indianapolis where he began life as a struggling lawyer. In 1856, despite advice from his father, he joined the newly formed Republican party. By 1860 he was successful at both law and politics, having been elected to the fairly lucrative position of Indiana Supreme Court reporter. In 1862 he left to join the Army. Harrison's profession and his religion and the seriousness with which he pursued one and followed the other gave him a consistency rare among men.

●**Residences:** Benjamin was born at North Bend. He grew up at the point, near the riverfront west of Cincinnati. He moved to Indianapolis at age 20 and lived in several homes there.

●**Personal Characteristics:** Harrison was about 5' 7", with light hair, fair skin, and blue eyes. Publicly he was always serious, hardworking, and disciplined. His lack of personability and inexpressiveness for small talk led some to call him a human iceberg. His speeches were logical and legalistic. At times, however, he could be deeply emotional, even poetic. People supported him because of his speaking ability, logical way of thinking, his honesty and integrity. To the outside world he was respected but never beloved.

～

I. Harrison In The Civil War:

*I am not a Julius Ceasar, nor a Napoleon, but a plain Hoosier colonel
with no more relish for a fight than for a good breakfast.*
—Before the siege of Atlanta, August 20, 1864

The timing of the Civil War was not propitious for Harrison. He had bought a house for his young family and he was finally making money. But he strongly believed in the United States and the anti-slavery cause, and it was hard for him to resist Lincoln's call for troops. With the encouragement of Indiana Governor Oliver Perry Morton and others, Lincoln had issued additional calls for volunteers. Indiana and Ohio in 1861 had greatly exceeded their quotas so in 1862 the response was much slower. Morton expressed dismay to Harrison and Harrison agreed to use his speaking ability to help raise troops. Morton suggested that he raise a regiment and he be its colonel. Harrison said that he didn't know anything about the army but agreed to accept the position of second lieutenant. Harrison raised the 70th Indiana and William Wallace, his former law partner, was its first recruit. Upon its successful recruitment he was made captain and later colonel.

Like Hayes and Garfield, Harrison learned his military principles out of books. In addition, like the smart lawyer that he was, he hired a superb drillmaster from Chicago. He put all his considerable energy and zeal into making the 70th Indiana, "march, think and act as one." In August his unit was sent to Louisville, Kentucky. Their treatment there was much different than in Indianapolis. Mainly the blacks welcomed them. Quickly, they were sent to Bowling Green in southern Kentucky to guard the Louisville and Nashville Railroad from Morgan's Raiders. At Russellville, Kentucky on September 30, 1862, Harrison got his first taste of battle. He took 600 men from Indiana and Kentucky, repaired a burned bridge, and routed the enemy.

On another front, Generals Buell (USA) and Bragg (CSA) fought to a standoff at Perryville, Kentucky. Both sides were disappointed, the Confederates left Kentucky, and Rosecrans replaced Buell. In late November, Harrison's troops were sent to Gallatin, Tennessee. Harrison marched much of the way, letting the sick use his horse. In Murphreesboro Rosecrans fought the Battle of Stone River, a bloody victory for the U. S. Army, then began his six months of idleness that frustrated Garfield and eventually Grant. Harrison spent 1863 guarding railroads, chasing guerrillas, and drilling. In March of 1864, after Grant became commander of all U. S. Armies, Sherman was appointed to take the center: Chattanooga to Atlanta and later the march to the sea, cutting the Confederacy in half. The 70th Indiana was moved under "Fighting Joe" Hooker, as a part of General George Thomas's army under Sherman.

Joe Johnston, a cautious and clever Confederate strategist, had 70,000 troops to guard the 120 miles between Chattanooga and Atlanta. His plan was to build fortifications and play defense, waiting for Sherman to make a fatal mistake. Sherman with his 100,000 troops sought to outflank Johnston. The battles began south of Chattanooga, in Dalton, Georgia, and advanced toward Atlanta.

We have been having very warm weather for several days and the trees are bursting into full foliage as if by magic, after being kept back so long by the cold rains and winds. These steep and craggy sides of Lookout will soon be hidden by a leafy curtain. Is it not a strange contrast that while nature is budding into a sweet and joyous life, man should be preparing for a carnival of death?...I fancy these stalwart soldiers of the hillsides are unfurling their leafy banners to welcome us, and that the songsters in their branches are singing to cheer us, as we march on, the conquering soldiers of freedom...In nature there is no life except the seed be cast into the earth and die, and so in our national life, shall yet yield its fruit in a purer, higher and surer national life...May God help us who stand for our country in the coming conflict to quit ourselves like men.
   —Letter to Carrie, April 26, 1864

They fought at Dalton, Resaca, Cassville, New Hope Church, Golgatha (where Harrison ended up acting as a surgeon), Pickett's Mill, Dallas, Kennesaw Mountain. Generally, Johnston stood and fought while Sherman moved around a wing and Johnston withdrew to the next position. When his brigade chief was wounded Harrison led the brigade. Like Hayes, he was famous for leading his men; his call was "Come on," not "Go on." He was fearless and resourceful and winning the praise of his generals.

...As you have never seen one of these field works, I must try to give you an idea of what an assaulting column has to overcome. In the first place in advancing you will come at 1,000 yards from the enemy's works into a "tangle," that is, all the small trees and some large ones felled cross-wise so that you have to make your way through a continual succession of treetops. As you get nearer, say 300 yards, you come to an abatis which consists of treetops...bushy ends towards you, all the leaves trimmed off and every branch and twig sharpened...about 20 yards from the rifle pits two lines of stakes about twelve feet long set about four feet in the ground and inclining towards you, the upper end being sharpened and the stakes so close that a man can't pass between them. If you can stand the deadly stream of musketry fire until you can dig up or cut down these stakes, you will have no other obstacle save the climbing of the breastworks and a line of bayonets jutting up inside...they also have what the boys call "horse rakes" ... made by boring huge auger holes through logs 20 feet long or so, at right angles, and putting through them long oaken stakes or pines sharpened at both ends so that however many times you may turn the thing over, there is always an ugly line of sharpened stakes sticking out towards you.
   —Letter to Carrie, July 10, 1864

◀ *Harrison leads his brigade at the Battle of Resaca, May, 1864.*

On July 17 the Confederates replaced the cautious Johnston with the aggressive John Bell Hood. On July 20 Hood attacked a small gap in the Union line at Peach Tree Creek. Harrison and two other regimental leaders closed the gap, possibly saving a massive loss. Harrison was commended for his courage and initiative by Sherman and Hooker. The siege of Atlanta began in late July. Before Sherman encircled it, Hood burned Atlanta, withdrew, and headed for Nashville. Sherman sent Thomas and Schofield to stop him while he, himself, Sherman (with the 70th Indiana), headed for the sea. Harrison, now a hero, went home to Indianapolis to campaign for Lincoln and recruit more troops.

In the fall of 1864 in the Union, optimism was high. Sherman took Atlanta, Sheridan triumphed in the Shenandoah Valley, and Admiral Farragut won at Mobile Bay. The Republicans won in Indiana, and Harrison was reelected to his old position of Supreme Court reporter. Lincoln won nationally, and the war continued.

After his furlough in Indiana Harrison headed for Georgia to rejoin Sherman. The railroad in Georgia was torn up, and he was unable to get there. He was sent instead to Nashville where with 5,000 miscellaneous troops under General J. B. Steedman they joined forces against Hood. Hood was confronted by two armies: Schofield's and Thomas's. Hood's idea was to defeat Schofield before he could join Thomas in Nashville. But Schofield got past Hood to Spring Hill, Tennessee, and headed for Nashville. Hood followed. Schofield stopped at Franklin, eighteen miles south of Nashville, found a good position, and fortified it. Hood attacked and failed, losing over 6,000 men and twelve general officers (Schofield lost 2,000 men). After the battle Schofield advanced to Nashville and consolidated forces with Thomas. It was early December and the war was delayed because of bad weather. Harrison walked the picket line taking coffee to new troops, many of whom never forgot him. Grant kept pushing Thomas to fight. The weather cleared on December 13 and Hood's camp began to stir. Steedman, in charge of the left, ordered Harrison to construct the front line defenses. Many citizens of Nashville helped. On December 15 Harrison and his troops moved forward. They didn't take the enemy front lines, but they positioned themselves better to fight the next day. Hood reduced his line from six miles to three to concentrate his force better. The U. S. Army broke through and routed the Confederates. Hood's troops were slaughtered and his army ceased to be a force.

After the battle, Harrison was sent to rejoin Sherman. He caught up with him in Raleigh, North Carolina. There, in the strange quiet on the streets, he learned that Lincoln had been assassinated, that Lee had surrendered to Grant, and that Johnston would soon surrender to Sherman. The war was essentially over.

The Civil War called for a president who had faith in time, for his country as well as for himself; who could endure the impatience of others and bide his time. A man who could by strong but restrained diplomatic correspondence hold foreign intermeddlers and at the same time lay the sure basis for the Geneva award, a man who could in all his public utterances, while maintaining the authority of the national government, breathe an undertone of yearning for the misguided and the rebellious; a man who could hold the war and the policy of the government to its original purpose—the restoration of the states without the destruction of slavery—until public sentiment was ready to support a proclamation of emancipation; a man who could win and hold the love of the soldier and the masses of people; a man who could be just without pleasure in the severities of justice, who loved to forgive and pardon...Qualities of heart and mind combined to make him a man who has won the love of mankind. He is beloved. He stands like a great light-house to show the way to duty to all his countrymen and to send afar a beam of courage to those who beat against the winds. We do him reverence. We bless...the memory of Lincoln.
        —Harrison speech, Lincoln Day Banquet, Chicago, February 12, 1898

∼
II. Civil Life

Mill fires were lighted at the funeral pile of slavery. The emancipation proclamation was heard in the depths of the earth as well as in the sky; men were made free, and material things became our better servants.
        —Inaugural Address, March 4, 1889

After the war, Harrison returned to Indianapolis somewhat embittered. He was a man of deep conviction and passion. He had seen a lot of killing and suffering. He thought the Confederates were responsible for defending the morally indefensible institution of slavery, of causing the war through the Kansas–Nebraska Act, and other attempts to extend slavery. Like Grant, Hayes, and Garfield, he thought the Copperheads—and many Democrats— deliberately undercut the war effort. Younger and more passion-driven than the others, he would comfortably wave the "bloody shirt" at Democrats while providing all the support he could for veterans of the Union army.

His career was law. He returned to his workaholic ways as a lawyer and his job as Indiana Supreme Court Reporter (taken away from him for two years by the Democrats while he was at the front). He worked longer and harder than his opponents, mastered details of cases, and presented clearly his clients' positions. After local prosecutors unsuccessfully failed to convict a woman named Nancy Clem in a sensational murder case, he was hired as special prosecutor. He won the conviction, his legal fame becoming as great as his military fame. He got involved in the famous *Milligan* case, where Garfield assisted in establishing the principle that it was improper for Lambdin P. Milligan and his co-conspirators to be convicted by a military court. The Supreme Court found that military courts did not have jurisdiction where civil courts were operating. It mandated damages against the military court officers. Milligan and his colleagues asked for $100,000. Harrison represented the military officers who ultimately had to pay $5.

In the meanwhile his eloquence as a speaker called him into every political campaign. In 1872 he lost the nomination as governor. In 1876 he was nominated but lost the election to James D. "Blue Jeans" Williams. Hayes wanted to appoint Harrison to a Federal office, but Morton, the boss of Indiana Republicans, vetoed that. In June of 1877, during the great national railway strike, Harrison organized a state militia to protect railroad property. Later, when the railroad union leaders were arrested, he pleaded successfully for their release and became a mediator between the parties. Although the railroad moguls were well tied to the Republican party, Harrison like Hayes, had sympathy for the workers.

In 1878, his father, John Scott Harrison died. In a bizarre development, his body was snatched and sold to the Medical College of Ohio in Cincinnati for research. Harrison's brother found the body, while looking for another.

While the Republican party may not always have been right, it has always been nearer right than any other party that existed contemporaneously...Even so the party has not always been successful in selecting the best men for offices and public trusts...
—Speech to the Young Man's Republican Club, Indianapolis, March 9, 1880

In 1877 Morton died and Harrison became leader of the Indiana Republicans. In 1880, after a deadlock at the Republican convention, he threw Indiana's support to Garfield and helped him win the nomination for the Presidency. Garfield also wanted to appoint him to a Federal office, but the Indiana legislature elected him as senator.

Don't let us be afraid of the people.

—Concluding remarks, acceptance of senate seat, January 11, 1881

There is no better school for the cure of modesty than Washington.

—Letter to John Morris, March 29, 1886

The issues during Harrison's senate term were Civil Service reform and the tariff. He supported the Civil Service reform by voting for the Pendleton Act. This act, sponsored by Senator George H. Pendleton of Ohio, established a Civil Service Commission to draw up and administer examinations for the selection of certain Federal employees on a merit basis. Harrison voted against the Tariff of 1883 which reduced tariff rates five percent.

Parody of Harrison pondering upon a midnight weary

In addition he was an advocate for pension liberalization for U. S. Army veterans and against the Chinese Exclusion Act (a violation of our treaties, like breaking a contract); he favored a strong Navy and the setting aside of land for what would become national parks.

In 1884 the Democrats nominated as President a reform prosecutor from upstate New York, Grover Cleveland. The Republicans nominated their beloved, charismatic but morally tarnished senator from Maine, James G. Blaine. Cleveland won. In 1886 the Democrats gained control of the Indiana Legislature, and Harrison in a close election lost his senate seat. In 1888 the Democrats renominated Cleveland, who proved to be a cantankerous man of integrity. The Republicans, desperate to regain the White House, nominated their own cantankerous man of integrity, Benjamin Harrison. In a close election, Cleveland won the popular vote, but Harrison won the electoral vote and was elected President. The main issue of the election was the tariff.

Providence has given us the victory.
—Harrison to Republican Chairman, Matthew Quay,
December 1888

He ought to know that Providence hadn't a damn thing to do with it.
—Matthew Quay, Republican political boss, to journalist A. K. McClure, est. April, 1889

~

III. Harrison as President

Fellow Citizens: There is no constitutional or legal requirement that the President shall take the oath of office in the presence of people, but...The oath taken in the presence of the people becomes a mutual covenant. The officer covenants to serve the whole body of the people by a faithful execution of the laws so that they may be the unfailing defense and security of those who respect and observe them, and that neither wealth, station, nor the power of combinations shall be able to evade their just penalties or to wrest them from a beneficent public purpose to serve the ends of cruelty or selfishness.
—Inaugural Address, March 4, 1889

The inaugural address was typical Harrison. Note that he speaks of a covenant. This comes from both the religious and legal sides of Harrison. It harkened back to John Calvin, founder of Puritanism and lawyer; the Scottish Covenanters; and even the Old Testament Hebrew covenants with God. A covenant is a contract, a fundamental part of English and American law. Thus the serious Harrison pledged both a professional and personal commitment to the American people.

The address covered several themes. He chided great corporations for their violations of laws. He chided the "educated and influential classes" for their selective compliance with laws, and the effect of such selective compliance on the "ignorant classes." Finally he stated his conclusion that the United States has been specially blessed but reverted back to his idea of a covenant, that such blessings were bestowed upon the condition that "justice and mercy shall hold the reins of power, and that upward avenues of hope shall be open to all our people...."

Although it seems odd to read about the "educated and influential classes" and the "ignorant classes," the speech is remarkable: it resembles the speeches of the nation's founders and yet its issues are contemporary.

After assuming office one of Harrison's first actions was to name James G. Blaine as Secretary of State. This offended one faction of his party. He immediately offended most of the rest of his party by naming a strong and mostly independent cabinet. In his cautious way he supported Civil Service reform (appointing the mercurial Theodore Roosevelt as a Civil Service commissioner). He also supported the creation of two national parks, Yosemite and Sequoia, the Sherman Anti-Trust Act*, and, in a political compromise, the Sherman Silver Purchase Act. Both acts were named for Senator John Sherman, influential senator from Ohio. The anti-trust act was the first act directed against industrial combinations. Unfortunately it suffered from vagueness and was applied against labor unions as well as industrial "trusts."

The Sherman Silver Purchase Act was a mildly inflationary act providing for the government to purchase a fixed amount of silver each month. It served to weaken the gold standard and allow the greater issuance of paper money.

Harrison's fatal political act was his support for the McKinley Tariff, the highest tariff in our history. It raised prices for almost everyone and was very unpopular, causing the Republican loss of the House in 1890 and probably Harrison's re-election in 1892.

In foreign and defense matters, consistent with the recommendations of Admiral Alfred Mahan, he, and his Secretary of the Navy, Benjamin F. Tracey, supported increased appropriations for the Navy. During the Harrison Administration, the United States narrowly averted wars with Italy (based on lynching of Italians in New Orleans) and with Chile (murder of American sailors in Valparaiso, Chile). He encouraged the annexation of Hawaii and the convening of the first conference with Latin American nations on trade and improved political relations. He disputed the slaughter of seals with Canada and Great Britain, and the colonization of Samoa by Bismarck's Germany.

---

*The Sherman Anti-Trust Act was written in response to the Standard Oil Trust and other powerful organizations that would use their pricing power to eliminate competition and then set whatever prices the market would bear. The Sherman Anti-Trust Act was hard to write, hard to pass, and hard to enforce. There are inherent problems defining markets, illegal procedures, and obtaining proof. This was true in 1889 and remains true today.

The President is not very popular with the members of either house. His manner of treating them is not at all that fortunate, and when they have an interview with him they generally come away mad....I think this is exceedingly unfortunate, because I am sure we never had a man in the White House who was more conscientiously seeking to do his duty.
—Solicitor General William Howard Taft to his father, June 16, 1890

Carrie Harrison made her own impact on Washington. Her artistic and musical temperament added much to White House life. She went through the White House attic, found old treasures, and began the tradition of White House china. She sought to have the White House expanded but had to settle for modernization. She made the White House a center of music and dancing (for the first time since the Polk administration forty years before). She supported many charities, including Johns Hopkins Medical School, providing that they admit women. Harrison's term was also the centennial of Washington's term; there was much interest in history, including that of the Revolutionary War. Carrie became a founding member and the first governor-general of the Daughters of the American Revolution.

Mr. Chairman and Comrades of the Grand Army of the Republic: I had impressions both pleasurable and painful as I looked upon the great procession of veterans which swept through the streets of this historic capital today; pleasurable in the contemplation of so many faces of those who shared together the perils and glories of the great struggle for the Union; sensations of a mournful sort as I thought how seldom we should meet again...

As I have stood at the great National Cemetery at Arlington and have seen those silent battalions of the dead, I have thought how swiftly the reaper is doing his work and how soon in the scattered cemeteries of the land the ashes of all the soldiers of the great war shall be gathered to honored graves. And I could not help to feel that in the sturdy tread of those battalions there was yet a strength of heart and limb that would not be withheld if a present peril should confront the Nation you love. And if Arlington is the death, we see today in the springing step of those magnificent battalions of the Sons of Veterans, the resurrection. They are coming to take our places; the Nation will not be defenseless when we are gone...
—Speech to G. A. R. National Encampment, Boston, August 12, 1890

In 1892 Harrison was not particularly liked by his party, just as Cleveland

Harrison: The human iceberg almost smiles. ▶

was not particularly liked by his. Blaine, resigning as Secretary of State, (his replacement was John W. Foster, grandfather of John Foster Dulles, another famous moralistic Presbyterian), made his fourth try for the Republican nomination but was defeated. Harrison was renominated. Cleveland and the first Adlai Stevenson were nominated by the Democrats for President and Vice-President. The Populist party nominee was James B. Weaver of Iowa, another ex-Civil War general. The big issue between the main parties was the McKinley Tariff. The Populists proposed a whole series of reforms to help farmers, laborers, and other ordinary Americans.

In late 1891 Carrie became seriously ill. In the spring of 1892 she was diagnosed as having "nervous prostration." In the summer of 1892 Harrison learned that Carrie had "consumption"—tuberculosis. In September this became known to the public. She died on October 25, 1892, after much suffering. Mourning her death, and out of respect, the candidates stopped campaigning. Cleveland won the election, becoming the only President to serve two non-consecutive terms. Weaver, the Populist, collected over one million votes and won twenty-two electoral votes. Harrison returned to Indianapolis.

~

IV. The Final Years, 1893–1901

Harrison was despondent over the death of Carrie. He was another of those strong nineteenth century men who could barely function without a good wife. He returned to the law and to some extent to politics. He also wrote articles and lectured at universities; He wrote two books. In 1896 there were strong rumors that he would marry his wife's younger sister, a respectable choice. Instead he shocked the general public and his children, who disowned him, by marrying Carrie's sister's daughter, a widow named Mary Scott Lord Dimmick who was 37. They had a daughter, Elizabeth, born in 1897.

From 1897 to 1899, consistent with his beliefs on international law, he represented Venezuela before an international tribunal in a boundary dispute with the British over British Guiana. He filed an 800-page brief and made a twenty-five hour oral presentation. Still the British won on a case probably decided on politics not merit.

In March 1901 Harrison contracted the flu. It turned into pneumonia, and he died quietly March 13, 1901.

...One of the characteristics of General Harrison always commanded my profound respect-his fearless independence and stand for what he believed to be right and just...A fearless man inwardly commands respect, and above every thing Harrison was fearless and just.

—James Whitcomb Riley's Eulogy on Harrison, March 16, 1901

Great Lives do not go out. They go on.

—Inscription on Harrison's monument, Indianapolis. The words were uttered by Harrison, August 20, 1891

●The Legacy of the Benjamin Harrisons

Harrison was born at the North Bend, Ohio, in the house of his grandparents, William Henry and Anna Symmes Harrison. The house burned down in 1855. The monument to William Henry and Anna Harrison is on the land where the house stood. The house where Benjamin Harrison grew up, "The Point," was located on the Ohio side of the point where the Great Miami enters the Ohio River. Unfortunately that home was torn down in 1959. The Harrison home in Indianapolis is one mile north of US 40 (Washington Street) at 1230 North Delaware Street. He and Carrie are buried at Crown Hill Cemetery in Indianapolis, which is east of Martin Luther King Jr. Street between 32nd and 42nd (north).

The White House in Washington, DC (burned by the British in the war of 1812 and rebuilt during the Monroe administration), was expanded during the administrations of the two Roosevelts and Truman. White House china, chosen by each new administration, is on display there. The Daughters of American Revolution effectively promotes and protects much of our history. Unfortunately, it made a very unwise decision in denying Marian Anderson, the great American contralto, who was black, use of its hall in 1939. Eleanor Roosevelt then arranged for Anderson to sing at the Lincoln Memorial, thereby creating one of the transcendent symbolic moments in our history. Johns Hopkins Medical School is considered to be one of the great medical centers of the world. This is at least partly because of Carrie Harrison and other women, who gave it conditional support at a crucial time in its history.

●Books Relevant to Understanding the Benjamin Harrisons

A. Biographical

•❖**Sievers, Henry J.** 1952. *Benjamin Harrison, Hoosier Warrior 1833–1865.* Chicago: Henry Regnery Company.

-1959. *Benjamin Harrison, Hoosier Statesman: From the Civil War to the White House 1865–1888;* New York: University Publishers Inc.

-1968. *Benjamin Harrison, Hoosier President: The White House and After.* Indianapolis: The Bobbs-Merrill Co.

-1969. *Benjamin Harrison 1833–1901, Chronology-Documents-Bibliographic Aids.* Dobbs Ferry, NY: Oceana Publications, Inc.

Sievers devoted twenty years of his life to write the only modern biography we have of Harrison. This neglect of Harrison is partly the result that he was beloved by few and partly the result that many of his papers were lost after his death. They were subsequently found and deposited in the Library of Congress.

•❖**Wallace, Lew.** 1888. *Life of General Ben Harrison.* Philadelphia: Hubbard Co.

This is a nineteenth century campaign biography, written by the Civil War general and author of *Ben Hur.* It was a quickly written work that covers Harrison's life only up to the 1888 presidential election. Wallace's brother was one of Harrison's law partners and both Wallaces knew Harrison well.

B. Non-biographical

●**The Holy Bible.** *Amos* est. 750 B. C. and *James* est. 100 A. D.

In his daily living Harrison probably took his religion more seriously than any other President. Part of his eloquence suggests *Ecclesiastes* or *Habakkuk.* His condemnation of the rich and selfish suggest influence by Amos and other Old Testament prophets. James condemned empty religion: "Faith without works is dead."

●**Dickens, Charles.** 1857. *Little Dorrit:* Baltimore: The Penguin English Library.

Dickens created memorable characters involved in politics, society, justice and law. He was extremely popular in the United States and Harrison was one of his readers.

●**Harrison, Benjamin.** 1897. *This Country of Ours.*

- 1901. *Views of an Ex-President.* Indianapolis: Bowen-Merrill Co.
These books by Harrison are hard to obtain. They, of course, are written in the more serious style of a lawyer rather than the more eloquent style of his speeches.

●**Kenyon, J. P.** 1968. *Stuart England.* New York: Penguin Books.
Harrison's moralistic zeal, courage, and simplicity brings to mind the "roundheads," independents and Presbyterians of the English (British) Civil War. They defeated the king's army, overthrew the king, and had great impact on British and American history. Kenyon's book is a straight-forward account of this dramatic period.

●**Lewis, Lloyd.** 1932. *Sherman, Fighting Prophet.* New York: Harcourt, Brace and Co.
This is a dramatic biography of a man who led a dramatic life and for much of Harrison's army service was his commanding general.

●**Mahan, Alfred T.** 1898. *The Influence of Seapower upon History 1660-1783.* Boston: Little, Brown and Co.
Mahan was our greatest naval theorist. His articles and books had great influence on Harrison and many others and resulted in changes in our national policy.

●**Sherman, William Tecumseh.** 1875, revised 1885. *Memoirs.* Current Edition 1990, New York: The Library of America, Literary Classics of the United States.
This is Sherman in his own words.

William McKinley

Graceful Conservative

25th President
March 4, 1897-September 14, 1901

He was a naturally kind and dutiful man. That, his common sense, discretion, and diligence took him far. He enlisted in the army for the Civil War as a private. He survived four years of combat, impressing many up and down the ranks, ending the war a major. He never talked about the glories of war. In marriage made difficult by tragedy he demonstrated time and again his kind and dutiful nature. Politically he had his opponents but worked easily with all. His issue became the tariff. He thought it helped industry *and* workers. It also generally kept him out of the controversial currency questions. He rose to the Presidency. There, he was confronted by a clamor for war. He refused to be stampeded. Why? Perhaps the kind and dutiful man did not want others to go through what he went through. We'll never know. The end was typical: he worried about his assailant; he worried about his wife. He died as he lived: a kind and dutiful man.

What doth the Lord require of thee, but to do justly, and to love mercy, and to walk humbly with thy God?
—A favorite passage of McKinley's from *The Bible*, Micah 6:8

◀ *He was the last Civil War veteran in the White House and saw an expanded American influence.*

●**Family Heritage:** McKinley was born January 29, 1843, in Niles, Ohio, the seventh of eight children of William McKinley and Nancy Allison McKinley. The early McKinleys, from Perthshire, Scotland, settled in Ireland, and later emigrated to York County, Pennsylvania. William's great great grandfather, a weaver, and great grandfather, both fought in the Revolutionary War. His grandfather fought in the War of 1812 under William Henry Harrison. He settled in New Lisbon, Ohio, where he started an iron business. William's father, William (Sr.), entered the iron business as a teenager. The family later moved to Niles where William (Jr.) was born and then Poland, Ohio, where William grew up. William's father was versatile, hard-working, and generally successful. His mother was well-organized and a key member of the local Methodist church. The McKinley children saw the necessity of hard work and duty but also were good humored.

●**Religion:** McKinley was raised a Methodist. His mother had hoped William would grow up to be a Methodist minister. Religion remained important to him all his life.

●**Education:** McKinley attended a public school in Niles, Ohio. Later the family moved to Poland, Ohio, to take advantage of a private New England-type high school run by the Methodists. McKinley was interested in the Everett Debating Society of Poland where he learned to be an effective speaker. At age 17 he entered Allegheny College in Meadville, Pennsylvania. McKinley, one of the healthiest men ever to serve as President, suffered a physical breakdown, probably from overwork, and dropped out of college because of that and the economic depression that began in 1857, which created difficult times for his family. He taught school for one year in Poland, Ohio, and clerked in the post office until he volunteered for the army. After the Civil War he apprenticed in the Youngstown law office of Judge Charles Glidden and attended law school in Albany, New York, for two terms.

You are the only man of all that have sought her that I would have given her to.
   —Ida Saxton's father, James, to William McKinley

●**Wife:** McKinley married Ida Saxton, a pretty, refined, demanding, high-strung, and indulged daughter of a well-to-do Canton banker, on January 25, 1871. They had two children that died as infants. That and the death of her mother in the same time period caused Ida to become an invalid the rest of her life. Sickness was not often talked about in the nineteenth century, and when Ida had periodic epileptic seizures or fainting spells McKinley would cover them up as if nothing had happened.

Ida, McKinley's First Lady

●**Personal Characteristics:** McKinley was good natured, optimistic, yet also fatalistic. He was reserved, modest, and somewhat stoical, never talking about certain personal things. He liked people and communicated that well. He had common sense and a practical way of solving problems. He was a good listener, observing people carefully. He concentrated on long term objectives, working intuitively and by indirection, which led impatient people, like Theodore Roosevelt, to criticize him. McKinley, like Lincoln, would listen to advice and make the decisions when he was ready. This made him a good strategist and negotiator.

~

I. The Civil War: From Private to Major, 1861–1865

On the following night, four of us volunteered to go out and catch the "seceshers"
if possible. Accordingly we started out about dusk led by a certain lieutenant of our regiment.
It would have done your heart good to have seen the above lieutenant prodding the bushes with
his gilded sword, fancying that he saw the hideous monster in the shape of a rebel. Ah,— the
ambitious officer was disappointed; instead of sticking a secesh, he without doubt stuck a skunk.
We came to this from the fact that a strong smell issued from the bushes....
—McKinley to W. K. Miller, August 11, 1861

McKinley enlisted with the 23rd Ohio as a private in June of 1861. He and his cousin William Osborne characterized their decision to join as "cold blooded," *i.e.,* calculated rather than emotional. He was 18 years old, and he assured his mother he would return. He served until July of 1865 without being wounded or even becoming seriously ill.

Originally, McKinley found the army boring. He looked for things to do and became a clerk under Major Rutherford B. Hayes. Hayes found him bright and diligent and arranged his promotion to corporal, then sergeant, where he became responsible for supplies and food.

The initial battles of the 23rd were in western Virginia, a challenge physically and logistically. The troops won a small battle at Carnifax Ferry that built their confidence. In 1862 they rode the railroad from Parkersburg (now West Virginia) to Washington. There, they joined McClellan's troops for the Battles of South Mountain and Antietam in Maryland. At Antietam the front line troops, hungry and tired from the Battle of South Mountain, were fighting at Burnside Bridge, one of the crucial points of the battle. McKinley, ignoring the fire, drove a wagonload of hot food to the troops. Typically for McKinley, he was admired for this by both the troops and his superiors. Hayes nominated him to become a lieutenant in September of 1862. On his only furlough he went home to recruit additional troops.

At Kernstown in the Shenandoah Valley, McKinley led a small battalion to safety and later prevented artillery pieces from falling into enemy hands. In September at the Battle of Opequon, he was a captain on the staff of General Crook. At Cedar Creek, while tending an artillery piece, he helped General Sheridan find General Crook before Sheridan reformed the troops for victory. For his courage and leadership at Opequon, Fisher's Hill, and Cedar Creek, McKinley was made a brevet (temporary) major. He left the Army after the war at age 22.

McKinley, who served as a private or a non-commissioned officer for eighteen months, saw more front line duty than any U. S. President. With modesty and stoicism, he said little about his Army service. Although he remained as kind and thoughtful as ever, it is likely that his memories of death in the Civil War had a great impact on his character.

II. McKinley after the War, 1865–1877

You know, at times, I am in imagination somewhat flighty, I have gotten over all that.
(I) am now a "rustic youth" wrapped in the mysteries of law. The "solemnities" of the
"marriage contract," the old customs of the Saxons and the Danes are constantly flitting
through my brain. I dream of lands, tenements and heriditaments, and wake up (to) think
I am an heir. Isn't that strange! I am getting along much better than I expected; Poland
is very tame, but I have banished myself.
    —Letter to Russell Hastings, August 28, 1865

McKinley returned to Poland, Ohio, to read law under prominent Youngstown lawyer, Charles Glidden. Glidden was impressed and suggested McKinley attend law school. He attended Albany Law School in New York for six months where he worked hard and enjoyed the social life.

After law school, McKinley left Poland for Canton, a larger, more diversified city where his sister, Anne, was teaching school. He practiced law on his own until he was recruited by a prominent Democrat, Judge Joseph Belden, to become his partner. He worked hard at law and was moderately successful. Not unexpectantly, he was also successful socially. He got involved politically by campaigning for his former commander, Rutherford B. Hayes, who ran successfully for governor of Ohio in 1867. The next year McKinley organized a Grant Club in Canton and in 1869 McKinley ran for and won the job of prosecuting attorney of Stark County. As prosecutor, he prosecuted violations of the liquor laws, most famously at Mount Union College in Alliance.

McKinley was regarded as a catch by the women of Canton. Although somewhat short, he was a handsome man, likable, a genuine war hero, and a lawyer-politician with good prospects. He fell in love with the beautiful, if willful, Ida Saxton. Ida's grandfather founded the Canton *Repository* in 1815. Her father, James, was a well-to-do local capitalist who indulged his favorite daughter.

I have a mind to get married—time 25th of next month—place Canton. It is
now settled that Miss Saxton and I will write our fortunes at the above time and place.
I of course am happy and want my friends to know it and therefor hasten to tell you....
    —Letter to Rutherford and Lucy Hayes, December 12, 1870

Like much of McKinley's life, his marriage was both dramatic and tragic.

McKinley promised voters "a full dinner pail."

The McKinleys were a handsome and joyful couple for two years, until they lost an infant daughter and Ida's mother in a short period of time. To deepen the tragedy their beautiful and bright 3 1/2-year-old daughter, Katherine, died suddenly of typhoid fever. Ida could not cope with the tragedies. She became a depressed, nervous invalid with severe headaches and epileptic seizures, never again to lead a normal life. McKinley, who had seen a lot of death, accepted the tragedies with stoicism. He had his work, his stimulating dealings with people, and his budding political career. However, he never neglected Ida. He took care of her with great kindness, no matter how busy he was. In those days, it was mentioned only that Mrs. McKinley was "sick" or an "invalid."

McKinley was always discreet in his private life, but many in Canton and elsewhere, recognizing his unselfish grace, found his treatment of Ida to be noble.

In March of 1876 there was a strike by miners in Tuscarawas County. The mine owners fought the strike and violence ensued. The strike leaders were arrested, and no local lawyer would take their case. It was a perfect case for the genuinely fair-minded McKinley. He pointed out the difficulties of the miners' plight and suggested that if the owners had been more responsive there would have been no strike and no violence. He got most of the strike leaders off and then refused to accept any fee for his work. The miners, mostly Democrats, long remembered this service. One of the representatives of the mine owners was Marcus Alonzo Hanna. Hanna, a clever businessman, concluded that such strikes were wasteful and needless and organized his enterprises to minimize the possibilities for such strikes.

In the summer of 1876, when Hayes was nominated for President, McKinley was nominated for Congress for a district involving Stark, Mahoning, Columbiana, and Carroll counties.

~

III. McKinley in Politics, 1877–1896

*The constant struggle all the time is anything but agreeable, but it seems necessary
to any success in life in anything. In politics it is a little more irritating than other things,
but I can stand it.*
      —Letter to brother, Abner McKinley, March 12, 1882

In the 1880's and 1890's, Ohio had three Republican political leaders of national importance: John Sherman of Lancaster and Mansfield, Joseph B. "Fire Alarm" Foraker of Cincinnati, and McKinley. Sherman was a serious candidate for President in 1880 and 1888. Foraker, a charismatic speaker, became governor of Ohio 1886-1890. McKinley was the quietest and most likable of the three. Marcus Alonzo Hanna, the talented Cleveland entrepreneur (born New Lisbon, Ohio) was also involved in politics. He eventually left business to devote full time to politics. His goal seemed to be to put an Ohioan who understood business in the White House. In 1888 he supported the irascible Sherman. For a while he supported Foraker until, after Foraker became governor, they had a falling out that resulted in a lifetime rivalry. Finally, he decided to support McKinley. They became a remarkable team. Both were sociable, listeners and watchers, rather than readers. McKinley was cautious, considerate, and honest with great political judgment. Hanna was an imaginative organizer and doer. Like most people, he liked McKinley. He also respected him for his honesty.

McKinley served 12 years in Congress: 1877-1883 and 1885-1891. He served in a swing district that was frequently gerrymandered. Since he was a good listener and a natural mediator, he was ideally suited to the district. He was a cautious conservative who supported some cheapening of the currency by voting for the Bland-Allison Act and the Sherman Silver Purchase Act. He also supported the Sherman Anti-Trust Act. (See page 103 for an explanation of these acts. The Bland-Allison Act, passed over Hayes's veto in 1877, was a mild compromise authorizing the purchase of silver and therefore the issuance of more money. It had minimal impact.)

McKinley thought the transcendent issue of the day was protectionism. He thought it would protect both owners and workers, uniting them under one national cause. It was also a great fund-raising aid for the Republican party that could encourage campaign contributions by businesses for their own protection. In 1890, during the Harrison administration, McKinley introduced a tariff bill.

His goal was to protect a few essential industries. There were many pressures in writing the bill. The business owners and associations who would be the chief beneficiaries overreached and it became the highest tariff with the broadest scope to that date in U. S. history, raising prices considerably. This was very unpopular and in the election of 1890 the Republicans lost both houses of Congress. One of the losers was McKinley. There is one footnote to the McKinley Tariff. James G. Blaine, Harrison's Secretary of State, convinced McKinley to insert a reciprocity clause, providing the President with power to reduce tariffs by mutual agreements with other countries. McKinley liked the idea and got a form of reciprocity in the bill. It is a principle still used in our trade negotiations.

Although he lost his Congressional seat in 1890, the next year thanks to Hanna's encouragement and support and a rousing speech by Foraker, McKinley was nominated and elected as governor of Ohio. He was a pragmatic reformer, obtaining improved safety standards for railroad workers, an excise tax on business, and a law providing for mediation between labor and businesses. His second term coincided with the great depression of 1893 and there was much strife and turmoil by strikers or those that were laid off or locked out. McKinley talked to labor and business leaders to encourage mediation. When the violence continued he called out an overwhelming force of the National Guard at Massillon, Athens, Glouster, and Corning. He justified this by using one of his rare references to the Civil War, stating that regiments are not so eager to fight when they are confronted by brigades. His firmness minimized violence in Ohio and his attempts to mediate and his attitude that workers were people deserving to be heard kept him reasonably popular with both sides.

As a result of the 1893 depression, McKinley, who had never paid much attention to money, was essentially bankrupted. He had co-signed notes for a friend, Robert Walker, a Youngstown banker and industrialist. The bankruptcy made him talk of quitting politics. Hanna and others formed a committee and began raising money to pay the debts. McKinley protested but an odd thing happened. When the national public learned that McKinley, too, had been caught in the great depression, they responded by sending contributions. While many politicians had gotten rich in public service, McKinley had gotten poor and his popularity had increased.

In 1896, by clever organization and management by both Hanna and McKinley, McKinley received the Republican nomination for President on the first ballot.

The campaign: McKinley promised stability, Bryan promised radical reform.

The humblest citizen of all the land, when clad in the armor of righteous cause, is stronger than all the hosts of Error!...You shall not press down upon the brow of labor this crown of thorns! You shall not crucify mankind upon this cross of gold!

——William Jennings Bryan, acceptance speech, Democratic nomination, Chicago, July 8, 1896

That what we call money, my fellow citizens, and with which values are measured and settlements made, must be as true as the bushel that measures the grain of the farmer, and as honest as the hours of labor which the man who toils is required to give.

——McKinley campaign speech, Knoxville, Pennsylvania, July 31, 1896

The election of 1896 was a watershed election. The country was still in a severe depression and people were desperate. Cleveland, an honest and stolid man, didn't know what action to take. McKinley wanted to bring back more protectionism, and prosperity. The Democrats nominated William Jennings Bryan,

36 years old, "the boy orator of the Platte." The Democrats were joined by James B. Weaver and the Populists, a great force in the rural areas of the South, Midwest, and West. Bryan's solution to the hard times was the issuance of more money, specifically the purchase and unlimited coinage of silver. Millions of debtors, many in the West, liked this idea. Debt holders, many in the East who were worried about the gold standard being undermined, did not like this idea. McKinley, who had no strong views on the issue, tried to straddle it by calling for a compromise: the issuance of both gold and silver currency, based upon international agreements. Bryan, handsome, energetic, and charismatic, for silver, and the "gold bugs" of the East forced McKinley to take a stand. Finally he came out for gold. Both parties split. The "silver" Republicans of the West, who dramatically left the party at the convention, supported Bryan. The "gold" Democrats formed their own party, nominating former U. S. Civil War general, John Palmer, for President, and former Confederate general, Simon Boliver Buckner, for Vice-President. Grover Cleveland, who took no public position on the election, privately supported the "gold" Democrats.

Bryan's tour of the country was described as being like a prairie fire. McKinley, like Garfield and Harrison, ran a front porch campaign. The Republicans, alarmed by Bryan's zeal, raised a fortune, using it for organization and publicity. Businessmen told workers to vote for McKinley. The election was close, with McKinley winning slightly more than fifty percent of the popular vote, with 7,000,000 votes. Bryan had 6,500,000 votes and the "gold" Democrats 500,000.

IV. McKinley as President, 1897–1901

Oh, God, keep him humble.
 —Mother McKinley's prayer November 5,1896
after learning her son had been elected President.

I reluctantly take leave of my friends and neighbors, cherishing in my heart the sweetest memories and tenderest thoughts of my old home—my home now, and, I trust my home hereafter, so long as I live.
 —On leaving Canton, March 1, 1897

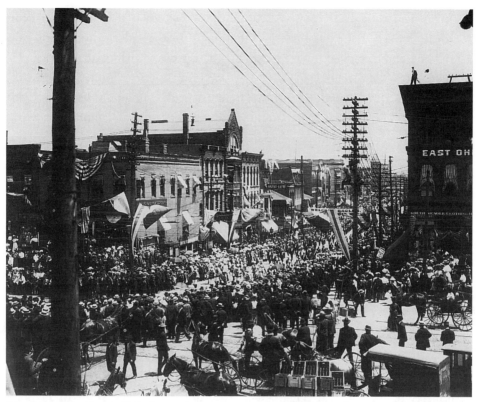

The celebration in Canton: McKinley won both majorities in popular and electoral votes, first time since Grant.

A. McKinley's Goals and Ideas

After the Civil War, the Republican party became strongly identified with the economic and industrial development of the country. This was natural for the party that mobilized the country for the war. One of the big issues continuously battled over was the value of money. Financiers, mostly in the East, wanted money to hold its value or appreciate. Debtors, often farmers, favored an "easy money" policy with credit widely available and debts easy to pay back. Hayes, who often looked at things in a moralistic way, intuitively thought the value of the dollar should not change. Garfield, the student and politician, studied everything he could about the issue, deciding mostly in favor of the high value of the dollar. McKinley, a natural conciliator, did not have strong views on the value of the dollar. His strong views were on the tariff. He thought it provided an umbrella for American industry *and* workers. He differed from many Republicans in his concern for the latter. As President, his views evolved. He saw the first task was replacing the Wilson-Gorman Tariff, passed during the Cleveland administration. Many thought the law brought on the depression of 1893. As President, McKinley looked at the issue afresh. He thought Blaine's idea of reciprocity was a good one, and he looked toward expanding it, especially with Latin America. He thought expanded foreign trade would be good for American industry and workers, as well as foreign nations and *their* industries and workers. He thought the increased world trading system could lead to greater political stability and world peace. America, whose industries had developed very successfully, no longer needed the same degree of protection it once did.

McKinley also began to diverge from his key supporter, Hanna. McKinley was not a trustbuster, but he never isolated himself from the concerns of ordinary people and he understood that the trusts would abuse their power at the expense of ordinary people. This violated McKinley's innate sense of decency and fairness. In his acceptance letter for the nomination in 1896 he characterized trusts as "dangerous conspiracies against the public good...that should be made subject of prohibitory or penal legislation...."

Not only did McKinley's and Hanna's political functions differ but so did their perception of the world. Hanna was a fund raiser, at times dealing with some rather reprehensible characters. McKinley was insulated from this, and while accepting and furthering Republican party principles he never condoned dishonesty or unfairness. When a scandal erupted involving some of Hanna's associates, and the American-run Cuban postal service, McKinley turned Joseph Bristow loose to prosecute the miscreants. Hanna was not happy.

Finally, McKinley, though tolerant of much human conduct, could not help but be appalled by some of the excesses of the Gilded Age. He retained the simplicity of a small town midwesterner. He was satisfied with a simple house and good company. He thought the Republican party, high tariffs and advanced industrialism, should give the advantages of prosperity to all.

B. The Spanish American War

I have seen war; I have seen the dead pile up, and I don't want to see another.
—Letter to General Leonard Wood, April 1, 1898

We want no wars of conquest, we must avoid the temptation of territorial aggression. War should never be entered upon until every agency of peace has failed; peace is preferable to war in almost every contingency.
—McKinley's Inaugural Address, March 4, 1897

1. Prelude to War

The question of fate comes up continually in history. Forces at work for years suddenly converge in crises, and an individual who has developed unique qualities turns out to have been exactly the right person for the times. Such was the case with Jefferson and the Declaration of Independence, Washington and the Revolutionary War, Lincoln and the Civil War, McKinley and the Spanish-American War. None of these men were perfect. All have been criticized for one thing or another. But looking back to what they accomplished is astonishing.

The seeds of the Spanish American war were in Spanish colonial policy. The Spanish had been exceptional explorers, creating a world-wide empire. Their rule, however, was often arbitrary and corrupt. Spanish colonies were characterized by a small, often arrogant elite and a large underclass without hope. The abuses of the Spanish colonial governments led to revolts and independence throughout Spanish America in the nineteenth century. Cuba had revolted unsuccessfully in 1812, 1868, and 1878. Under Jose Marti, Calexo Garcia, and others, they revolted again in 1895. At the other end of the world, the Filipinos, under the leadership of Emilio Aguinaldo, were revolting against the Spanish.

The stability of Cuba was a big issue with the United States. Under McKinley the Republicans looked outward for trade, and Cuba was one of the natural trading partners. The Spanish governments alternated between hard-line conservatives who cruelly repressed the Cubans and liberals who tried to ameliorate conditions with minor concessions. The Cuban *insurrectos* fought resourcefully and organized a propaganda arm in the United States. They communicated effectively with American newspapers, especially with the "yellow press" of William Randolph Hearst and Joseph Pulitzer who aired sensational charges that helped them sell more papers. Ultimately, their hope was for war. There was also a Republican wing, led by Senator Henry Cabot Lodge and Assistant Secretary of the Navy Theodore Roosevelt, that was eager to go to war. The latter, 40 years old in 1898, extremely energetic and egocentric, thought war would be good for American society. He was of questionable maturity at the time. (William James, a leading psychologist and philosopher, thought of Roosevelt as a perpetual adolescent.) Roosevelt thought it was the destiny of the United States to become a great power by throwing the Spanish out of the new world. He thought his own role would be that of a charismatic military leader. But he needed a war.

McKinley did all he could to avert war. He had pragmatic and personal reasons. Pragmatically, the war might harm Republican prosperity. Politically,

McKinley was always cautious. Personally, he had seen four years of brutal war, and he reacted matter-of-factly. Unlike his mentor, Hayes, he probably never thought of war as glorious. Like many things, it was a job to do, and he did it.

Cuba Libre!
    —A common slogan popular in America at the time

For the United States, the Cuban crises began in the Cleveland administration. Cleveland, whom McKinley liked, pursued a policy of neutrality towards the *insurrectos*. McKinley tried to maintain the policy of neutrality while trying to persuade the Spanish to follow more enlightened policies.

The Spanish were closely divided between hard-line conservatives and non-hard-liners. The Spanish colonial governor, "Butcher" Wyler, rounded up rural families and concentrated them in camps. The Cuban *insurrectos* destroyed crops and facilities in the countryside. Neither side could win. The American press relayed cruel stories, some of which were true. The Spanish conservatives fell, and Wyler was replaced. The Spanish military rioted in Havana, murdering dozens of people. To those that wanted to go to war, this seemed a perfect pretext. American consul Fitzhugh Lee asked that he have the option of ordering a naval vessel to protect American citizens. McKinley granted that authority. Then by agreement with Spain, McKinley sent the battleship *Maine* to Havana harbor.

At the same time, McKinley sought to work his famous charm on the Spanish ambassador, Dupay de Lome. De Lome, an aristocratic conservative, seemed impressed with McKinley. But he had already written to a friend in Cuba that McKinley was "a cheap vacillating politician." The letter was intercepted by the *insurrectos* and forwarded to the American press. The yellow press again called for war. The Spanish not only insulted the man and the office but the country as well. McKinley kept his cool, and de Lome resigned.

A week later, the *Maine* blew up in Havana harbor with a loss of 250 U. S. sailors. Theodore Roosevelt called it an act of treachery. The press screamed for war. McKinley prepared. He asked Congress for $50 million. He ordered the battleship *Oregon* from the Pacific around Cape Horn, and he asked a Navy commission to investigate the sinking of the *Maine*. Roosevelt was impatient with McKinley and said he had "the backbone of a chocolate eclair."

Lee concluded that the *Maine* had probably hit a mine and that the Spanish were probably negligent rather than willful. McKinley thought if so, the *Maine* issue could be settled by Spanish payment of reparations. He then put more pressure on Spain to end hostilities and work towards Cuban independence. He thought if they accepted immediately there was a chance to avoid war. But McKinley was losing his own party in the Senate.

On March 25 the commission turned in its report on the disaster. It said it believed there was an external explosion, which set off the *Maine's* own explosive magazines. This conclusion leaked to the press. One of the moderate papers, *The New York Times,* said that there was no turning back from war. Congress made speeches and prepared resolutions. At this late date, the Spanish accepted nearly all of McKinley's conditions. Still, Congress was adamant. McKinley asked the Pope to intervene. (Even the Germans were interested in a peaceful settlement because they coveted Spanish possessions in the Pacific). McKinley ordered the evacuation of U. S. citizens. Lee said he needed five days. Congress no longer trusted McKinley; a majority of the Senate was ready to declare war. In what would have been unprecedented in American history, McKinley considered vetoing a declaration of war.

The country should understand that we are striving to make our course consistent not alone for today, but for all time; the people must not be unreasonable.
—Comment to assistant George Cortelyou, during the crises leading to war

On April 9, Spain conceded on all points. It was too late. The Senate had passed four resolutions: immediate Cuban independence, Spanish relinquishment of its American colonies, recognition of the *Insurrectos* as the legitimate government of Cuba, and U. S. military support of the resolutions. McKinley thought it inappropriate that the United States name the government of Cuba and got substituted the Teller amendment, which said the United States had no desire to govern Cuba. The war began April 21.

You may fire when ready, Gridley.
—Commodore Dewey to Captain Gridley at the Battle of Manila Bay, May 1, 1898

2. The War

While American newspapers and the public concentrated on Cuba, Spain, once the world's greatest imperial power, was vulnerable, not only in Cuba but

Under McKinley, the United States became a world power.

Puerto Rico, the Philippines, and in scattered islands like Guam. The United States began reaching into the Pacific by annexing the Hawaiian Islands in 1898 after an American-led revolution overthrew Queen Liliuokalani. This gave the U. S. Pearl Harbor, a key strategic port for action in the Pacific.

As assistant secretary of the Navy, Theodore Roosevelt, thinking globally, arranged that Commodore George Dewey be made head of the Pacific fleet. While Secretary of the Navy John D. Long was on leave, Roosevelt also gave Dewey specific instructions on taking the fleet to Hong Kong and making its ultimate target the Spanish fleet in the Philippines. This was a logical thing to do and his orders were not countermanded, but he was personally chastised by the gentlemanly Long for his improper assumption of authority.

When the war began Dewey was forced to leave Hong Kong, then under British control, so he sailed for Manila Bay where he attacked and destroyed the Spanish Pacific fleet. The U. S. Navy had one fatality, a heart attack by a ship's engineer, and Dewey became a great national hero.

While the Navy was winning glory, the Army was trying to get started. Its first job was to scale up from 28,000 to eventually 250,000 men. It was not easy or quick, its procedures were entangled in red tape, and its weapons were often obsolete. Just as in the Civil War, there were many volunteers to be generals. McKinley and Secretary of War Russell A. Alger faced the daunting task of picking them. McKinley had learned the lessons of the Civil War, and he tried to appoint all the top generals by merit. By stroke of political genius he picked two ex-Confederates, "Fighting Joe" Wheeler and the ex-representative to Cuba,

Fitzhugh Lee. Alger, a Michigan lumber magnate and former volunteer general in the Civil War, with a war record open to some question (and brother of successful inspirational writer, Horatio Alger), had his hands full naming the other officers. Among those named were Lieutenant Colonel Theodore Roosevelt and Colonel William Jennings Bryan.

The leaders of the army were Nelson A. Miles, the vain and ambitious "boy" general from the Civil War, and William R. Shafter, a gruff, unwieldy but competent general who weighed more than 300 pounds. Miles and Alger did not like each other and did not communicate well. For the Navy the Atlantic fleet was under the capable leadership of Rear Admiral William T. Sampson. Its job was to blockade Cuba. There was also a "flying squad" that patrolled the Atlantic and adjacent waters under Commodore Winfield Scott Schley. Schley had been involved in the incident at Valparaiso, Chile, during the Harrison administration that almost led to war. He had also rescued a polar explorer and written a book about it. The flying squad's job was to protect the Atlantic and Gulf coast cities from attacks by the Spanish Atlantic fleet.

Miles announced that he would hold off any invasion of Cuba until the rainy (and yellow fever) season ended. He would train his troops and straighten out his logistics. This surprised Secretary of War Alger and chagrined Secretary of Navy Long. They knew public pressure would demand action, and Miles ultimately agreed to a small invasion on the south coast of Cuba.

Theodore Roosevelt, aching for action, recruited a regiment of volunteers, eastern bluebloods, western cowboys, and Indians. They served under the remarkable former White House physician and military leader, Colonel Leonard Wood. Impatient with bureaucratic procedures and a master of using the press, Roosevelt became the most famous military leader to come out of the war.

To replace the *Maine*, the battleship *Oregon* was ordered to steam from Bremerton, Washington, to Key West, Florida, a journey of 8,000 miles around the treacherous Cape Horn. This made a compelling argument for a canal through Central America. The Spanish fleet had been ordered to the west, and the U. S. Atlantic fleet went looking for it. The Spanish fleet ended up in Santiago Harbor on the southeast coast of Cuba, the Navy blockaded the harbor, and it was there that the Army decided to invade.

Using the *insurrectos* for intelligence and to harass the Spanish Army, the U. S. Army made uncontested landings at Daiquiri and Siboney. The Marines at nearly the same time seized Guantanamo, one bay over, for a naval supply base.

Battles were fought at the crossroads of Las Guasimos, El Caney, Kettle Hill, and San Juan Hill. They were not easy fights, and only the refusal to quit saved the day. Roosevelt valiantly led his Rough Riders up the latter two hills where they were joined by the Ninth Cavalry, a troop of regular army black soldiers. Although the battle would scarcely compare to the smallest battles of the Civil War, Roosevelt received appropriate glory for his leadership. The 300-pound Shafter had been prostrated by the heat and gave orders while lying on a door. "Fighting Joe" Wheeler, the ex-Confederate general, got so excited at routing the Spanish, he exclaimed, "Come on boys, we got the Yankees on the run!"

The Spanish fleet was ordered to try to break through the American blockade, which it did while Admiral Sampson was heading for a meeting with Generals Miles and Shafter. Sampson didn't get back and the American fleet, using his plans but under the command of Schley, destroyed the Spanish fleet. Shafter and Miles then asked the Spanish to surrender Santiago. After much negotiation the Spanish did. The U. S. agreed to ship 25,000 Spanish troops back to Spain.

Miles, looking for battlefield glory, invaded Puerto Rico. The troops were generally welcomed, and there were few fights. In the Pacific an American ship sent to re-enforce Dewey captured Guam. When the ship fired its shells, the small Spanish garrison thought the ship was saluting. When the garrison learned it was being attacked it surrendered.

The Philippines became a quagmire. The U. S. and the Philippine guerrillas easily took Manila from the Spanish. When the Spanish agreed to a peace treaty, it ceded the Philippines to the United States. This angered native leader Aguinaldo and his guerrillas who proclaimed their own Republic. Aguinaldo did not want to exchange one colonial power for another so the U. S. fought the guerrillas, getting in the uncomfortably ironic position of trying to save a country by fighting its own people. This was a tough little war lasting until March of 1901 when Aguinaldo surrendered. The United States pledged to give the Philippines independence, "when they were ready." McKinley also sent the talented and humane William Howard Taft there as governor-general.

C. The Post War Situation

The Spanish-American War profoundly changed America. Northern and Southern states, fighting for a common cause, developed a greater unity. America became a recognized power in the Atlantic and the Pacific, and when the major European powers devastated themselves in World War I, the United States was to become the pre-eminent nation in the world. The chronically disorganized U. S.

McKinley: "I have had all the honor there is in this place..."

Army was reorganized under the bright and practical Elihu Root, successor to Secretary of War Alger. The scourge of yellow fever was successfully attacked in Cuba by a team of army doctors led by Dr. Walter Reed. This was a major disease throughout the tropics and one factor in preventing the French from completing their canal through Central America. Finally, as an extension of the policy in the Philippines, McKinley brought the brilliant and erudite John Hay home from his job as envoy to London to become Secretary of State.

Hay announced and cleverly executed the Open Door policy on free trade by all nations with China. He also directed American participation of the lifting of the siege after fifty-five days at Peking (Beijing) during the Boxer Rebellion, a native revolt against foreign influence in China.

Cuba, granted its independence, seemed to copy Spain politically, alternating between liberalism and dictatorship. In 1959 its last right-wing dictator, the cruel and corrupt Fulgencio Batista, was overthrown by left-wing dictator Fidel Castro. The U. S. retains its base at Guantanamo and Puerto Rico became a U. S. commonwealth with a future yet to be determined.

The Philippines, after they were conquered by the United States in its forgotten war, became a key battle area in World War II—Luzon, Bataan, Corregidor, Leyte. They gained their independence on July 4, 1946. They are a diverse country that had some of the worst traditions of Spanish colonial government. In 1965 Ferdinand Marcos took over. He was ruthless and corrupt and was eventually overthrown in 1986. Guam and other Mariana islands, Tinian and Saipan, were also battlegrounds in World War II. Guam remains a U. S. territory. Guamians and Puerto Ricans are U. S. citizens.

D. The Election of 1900

The election of 1900 was between the two main adversaries from 1896. Prosperity had returned to the land and this was in the Republicans' favor. Gold had been discovered in the Klondike of Alaska, and there was more credit available to a growing and prosperous nation. Bryan insisted on making an issue of silver, which likely harmed his chances. Some Democrats made an issue of imperialism, but McKinley's handling of the war was popular and the people were willing to trust him. The nominated Vice-Presidents were different. Garrett Hobart, a decent and reasonable man whose wife greatly helped Ida McKinley, died in office during McKinley's first term. The first Adlai Stevenson, one of Cleveland's Vice-Presidents, was nominated by the Democrats. McKinley wanted Senator William B. Allison of Iowa, but Allison refused the nomination. He then accepted Theodore Roosevelt, the well-publicized hero of the war. Roosevelt, a man of great energy, traveled around the country doing most of the campaigning, and the Republicans won a bigger majority than in 1896.

The second McKinley administration, beginning the first year of the twentieth century, did not last long. McKinley, a gifted, intuitive politician and a cautious, practical man with a generous nature, seemed to see the dim outlines of a new order in the world. It would be an interdependent world of lower tariffs and peace based upon international trade and growing democracy, its disputes settled by arbitration. It would be a precursor to the world economy recognized so widely in the latter part of the same century.

Part V. The McKinleys' Deaths

Early in his second term McKinley, always refreshed by crowds, undertook a western trip. During the trip, Ida got blood poisoning from a minor infection, which threatened her life. Funeral plans were made, when to the immense relief of her husband, she rallied and eventually recovered. They returned to Washington, and he scheduled a trip to the Pan-American Exposition in Buffalo, New York, in September of 1901. While there, he was shot by an anarchist. Thoughtful to the end, he instructed them not to hurt the gunman. His second thought was for Ida: "My wife, be careful, Cortelyou, how you tell her." He died eight days later. Ida moved back to Canton where she lived until May 26, 1907.

McKinley Memorial, Canton, Ohio   118424-N

The McKinley Memorial: He was at the height of his Presidential popularity when he was shot.

*The rainbow of hope is out of the sky. Heavy clouds hang about us. Tears wet
the grounds of the teepees. The palefaces too are in sorrow. The Great Chief of the Nation
is dead. Farewell! Farewell! Farewell!*
    —Wording on a card from an anonymous American Indian at Buffalo

●McKinley Legacies

The McKinley legacies, like those of Grant, are complicated. He was a naturally kind and sympathetic man. He began the Civil War as an ordinary private and no matter how high he rose in politics he never forgot ordinary people. Politically he was no intellectual like Hayes or Garfield or even Harrison. In Congress he was a practical politician who focused mainly on one issue: the tariff. It is ironic that he totally lost control of the bill that bore his name. As governor of Ohio during a depression he acted decisively for public order but met continually with both sides. As President his finest hour was his refusal to be stampeded by popular will into war. He was one of a small minority who understood first-hand what war was. Finally, McKinley, like Rutherford Hayes and Benjamin Harrison, appointed some of the most talented government leaders that the country has ever had, including John Hay, Secretary of State, Elihu Root, Secretary of War,

131

John Griggs and Philander Knox as Attorney Generals, William Howard Taft as Governor of the Philippines, and James Wilson (father of scientific farming) as Secretary of Agriculture. Harrison and McKinley both, of course, appointed Theodore Roosevelt to positions.

●Visiting McKinley Sites

There is a small classical Greek birthplace memorial museum in Niles. The four McKinleys are buried in Canton in a spectacular monument modeled on Hadrian's tomb in Rome. The monument and grounds are shaped like a sword in a hilt. This alone is worth a trip to Canton. The nearby Museum of History, Science and Technology contains some items related to McKinley. Finally, the Church of the Savior United Methodist at Cleveland Avenue and Tuscarawas Street contains four glass windows presented by Ida McKinley, and the pew where the McKinleys sat while attending church there.

●Works Relevant to Understanding the McKinleys

A. Biographical

●❖Gould, Lewis L. 1980. *The Presidency of William McKinley.* Lawrence, KS: University Press of Kansas.
This book in the Kansas series covering many of the Presidents is fair and scholarly.
●❖Leech, Margaret. 1959. *In the Days of McKinley.* New York: Harper and Brothers.
Like all of Leech's books this is interesting. She effectively covers McKinley's relationships, especially with Ida, and the atmosphere in Washington during McKinley's years there.

●❖Morgan, H. Wayne. 1963. *William McKinley and His America.* Syracuse, NY: Syracuse University Press.
This is a good book. Morgan has more on McKinley's Civil War experience and less on Ida than Leech.

B. Non-biographical

1. The Spanish-American War

●**Freidel, Frank.** 1958. *The Splendid Little War.* Boston: Little, Brown and Co.
The title uses ironically the phrase coined by John Hay in a personal letter to Theodore Roosevelt. The book dramatically covers the war, using words and pictures from famous correspondents like Richard Harding Davis, Stephen Crane, John T. McCutcheon, Howard Chandler Christy, Frederick Remington, William Glackens, and future military and political leaders like John J. Pershing, William Leahy, Frank Knox, and Theodore Roosevelt.

●**Keller, Allan.** 1969. *The Spanish-American War; A Compact History.* New York: Hawthorn Books, Inc.
The war was short and this book generally covers it adequately although it could use more and clearer maps. McKinley and his administration are not put into a very clear context. For example, it is wrong to put Secretary of the Navy John Long, who served the country well, in the same category as Secretary of State John Sherman, who unfortunately was at that point in time mentally enfeebled.

●**Roosevelt, Theodore.** 1899. *The Rough Riders.* New York: Charles Scribner's Sons.
This is the energetic and egocentric Roosevelt's description of his part in the Spanish-American War. It helped make him a national figure, Vice President, and President.

2. Other Relevant Books

●**Beer, Thomas.** 1929. *Hanna.* New York: Alfred A. Knopf.
This is not really a biography as such but an idiosyncratic book that explores Hanna and his surroundings. Beer's father, who worked for the New York Life Insurance Co., knew both McKinleys and worked in the political-financial world with Hanna.

●**Crane, Stephen.** 1895 *The Red Badge of Courage.* Widely available in paperback.
Although five U.S. Presidents served in The Civil War, only McKinley served

as a private. This short book is self-consciously written from the standpoint of a private in the Civil War. It is a masterful work of imagination, expression, and psychological insight.

●**Croly, Herbert.** 1912. *Marcus Alonzo Hanna, His Life and Work*. Macmillan Co., Reissued by Archon Books, Hampden, CT. 1965.

Croly, the author of *The Promise of American Life* (1909) a progressive manifesto, became an advisor to both Theodore Roosevelt and Woodrow Wilson. This is a well-written book completed soon after Hanna's death. It relied on extensive contemporary interviews as well as some documentary evidence. It explains Hanna and much of his milieu from his birth in New Lisbon, Ohio, through his resourceful business organization and management and his political involvement.

●**Hay, John Milton.** 1871. *Castillian Days*. Boston: James Osgood and Company.

John Hay, a native of Salem, Indiana, was McKinley's last and Teddy Roosevelt's first Secretary of State. At age 23, he and John Nicolay became personal secretaries to Abraham Lincoln. They jointly wrote a ten-volume history of Lincoln. Later Hay wrote novels, poetry, editorials, and edited the complete works of Lincoln. Prior to becoming Secretary of State he served in the diplomatic service under Hayes and Garfield where his gracious manners and erudition served the United States well. He had the misfortune of serving three Presidents that were assassinated—Lincoln, Garfield, and McKinley. This book is about his observations based upon his service in Spain. It was published twenty-seven years before the Spanish-American War.

●**Karnow, Stanley.** 1989. *In Our Image: America's Empire in the Philippines*. New York: Random House.

Karnow, a former *Washington Post* reporter, wrote a widely praised book on Vietnam. He gives good if somewhat cynical history of the Philippines. He is culturally critical of people like McKinley and Taft. I think he underestimates their political difficulties and genuine good will.

●**O' Toole, Patricia.** 1990. *The Five of Hearts: An Intimate Portrait of Henry Adams and His Friends, 1880-1918*. New York: Clarkson Potter Publishers.

This is a splendid book about John Hay his wife, Cleveland native Clara Stone; Henry Adams, the intellectual great grandson and grandson of Presidents;

Henry Adams's wife, Clover; and Clarence King, a charismatic scientist. Hay, a talented writer and conversationalist, had worked closely with Lincoln every day and probably never fully recovered from the shock of the Lincoln assassination. Henry Adams, bright and cantankerous, knew every President from Lincoln to Theodore Roosevelt and was not shy about expressing his opinions. Clover Adams's tragic death is memorialized by one of the most moving pieces of sculpture in America, "Grief," by Augustus Saint-Gaudens.

●**Sears, Stephen W.** 1983. *Landscape Turned Red: The Battle of Antietam.* New York: Warner Books.

More Americans were killed at Antietam than any other single day in *any* war. McKinley at the time was a 19-year-old mess sergeant in the U.S. Army's IX Corps. He survived withering fire to deliver food to front line troops at Burnside Bridge. In addition to McKinley, other participants on the side of the United States include future Supreme Court Justice Oliver Wendell Holmes, Jr., and Clara Barton, nurse and founder of the American Red Cross. This book effectively tells the story of Antietam.

William Howard Taft
Cautious Progressive

27th President
March 4, 1909–March 3, 1913
10th Chief Justice
June 30, 1921–February 3, 1930

People first remarked about his size: 6' 3"—he weighed what two ordinary men would. Then they noticed his good humor. He self-deprecatingly chuckled his way through life with a winsome style. He was an unusually jovial person. But underneath it all he was serious and sensitive. He thought the country would be saved by a fair and just administration of law. While young he set his sights on the Supreme Court but was diverted by other things. As President he did more for the Presidency than the Presidency did for him. In the end he got his wish, becoming Chief Justice of the Supreme Court. There, his greatest contributions were not legal but personal, administrative, and political. His humor and willingness to work harmonized a group of strong individualists; he reorganized the Federal justice system; and he helped the court fully achieve its rightful constitutional position of that as a third co-equal branch of government. Big man; big achievements.

Circumstances seem to have imposed something...of a trust on me personally.
—Letter to Theodore Roosevelt, June 30, 1906

◄ *Taft was a careful man in the White House and his real ambition was always the Supreme Court.*

137

●**Family Heritage:** William Howard Taft was born September 15, 1857, in Cincinnati, Ohio. "Will" was the oldest of four children of the second family of Alphonso Taft. Alphonso and his first wife, Fanny Phelps Taft, had two sons that survived, Charles Phelps Taft (the first) and Peter Rawson Taft. After Fanny died Alphonso married Louisa (Louise) Torrey. They had three sons and one daughter. The Tafts, the Phelps, and the Torreys (and the Howards) were all New Englanders of mostly English and some Scots-Irish descent. The Tafts had been involved in government from the early 1700's. Alphonso, a lawyer, and his two wives read widely and discussed history, various sciences, and literature. Louisa also played the piano. Alphonso, who was fiercely anti-slavery, became a founder of the Republican party in 1856. He served as a local judge, and as Secretary of War and Attorney General under Grant, and minister to Austria-Hungary and Russia under Arthur. The Tafts were not rich, but the children grew up in a nurturing environment. Louisa accepted her two stepsons as her own. Her unmarried sister, Delia, was close to all the children. Throughout their lives the family was affectionate to and supportive of one another.

●**Religion:** The Tafts, distant relatives of Ralph Waldo Emerson, became Unitarians. Will explicitly did not believe in the divinity of Christ. He was criticized for his beliefs when he ran for the presidency.

However different man and woman may be intellectually, coeducation...shows that there is no mental inferiority on the part of girls...Give the woman the ballot, and you will make her more important in the eyes of the world....Every woman would then be given the opportunity to earn a livelihood. She would receive no decrease in compensation for her labor on account of her sex....In the natural course of events, universal suffrage must prevail throughout the world.

—William Howard Taft, while a student at Woodward High School, est. 1874

●**Education:** Will was educated at the 16th district public school in the Mt. Auburn section of Cincinnati. He graduated from Woodward High School, Yale, and the University of Cincinnati law school. He was an outstanding student of math, composition, and physical education. He also went to dancing school and was always a good dancer, despite his size.

●**Wife:** In 1886 Will married Helen (Nellie) Herron, the daughter of a local judge who was a former law partner and good friend of Rutherford B. Hayes. She

PRESIDENT TAFT AND HIS FAMILY
IN THEIR WHITE STEAMER

When Yale offered Taft its Chair of Law, Taft declined. He said that his size required a "Sofa of Law."

was a graduate of the Cincinnati College of Music, well educated, forceful, and ambitious. She had taught school for three years. While a schoolgirl she visited the Hayeses at the White House and became rather enamored with Washington. The Tafts had three children, Robert A., who became a famous senator and leader of the Republican party; Charles Phelps (II) of Cincinnati, first lay leader of the Federal Council of Churches of America; and Helen Herron Taft Manning who became a history professor and dean at Bryn Mawr College in Pennsylvania.

I wonder Nellie dear, if you and I will ever be (in Washington) in some official capacity? Oh, yes, I forgot; of course we shall be when you become secretary of treasury.
    —Letter to Nellie March 6, 1886

●**Personal Characteristics:** As a child because of his size, strength, and good nature, he became somewhat of a mediator. As an adult he was a giant of a man, 6' 3", 240-336 lbs. One story had the President swimming at Beverly Bay, Massachusetts, in a bathing suit of mammoth proportions. Two of the neighbors approached for a swim but one of them suggested they wait. "The President is using the ocean," he said. Taft was a hard worker, modest, liked people, laughed a lot, and was respected by both parties for his honesty, integrity, and intelligence.

≈

I. Early Career, 1878–1892

I got my political pull, first, through my father's prominence: then through the fact
that I was hail-fellow-well-met.
> —Letter to William Allen White, February 26, 1908

After graduating from Yale, Taft returned to Cincinnati. While attending the University of Cincinnati law school he worked full time as a reporter for the Cincinnati *Commercial*. After completing law school he took a pay cut to become assistant prosecutor for Hamilton County. There, he first encountered his *bête noire*, Tom Campbell, an effective defense lawyer who used all the procedures available to him to aid his clients. After two years Taft was appointed tax collector for Ohio's first district (a job previously held by William Henry Harrison) by President Chester A. Arthur. He quit when Republican bosses wanted him to replace some of his best people with political hacks, and he began the practice of law.

There was a major case in Cincinnati in 1883 when two workers killed their boss, the owner of a livery stable. They took his money and lived it up at the local bars, were caught, and confessed. The local papers screamed about their guilt and demanded the death penalty. The family of one hired Tom Campbell as its defense lawyer. The charge was reduced to manslaughter, and the penalty was not the death sentence. The papers were incensed, and a mob formed. On the first night the authorities protected the jail (forty-two people accused of murder were in the jail). On the second night, the state militia was called out to protect the jail, but the mob burned the courthouse. The riot resulted in the deaths of forty-five people. Taft, who thought the law should punish miscreants and free the innocent, blamed Campbell.

Taft was appointed to a commission that sought to disbar Campbell. Taft lost the case but earned a certain local fame. In 1885 he became assistant solicitor general for Hamilton County. Two years later he was appointed as judge to the superior court by Governor Foraker, a man he didn't like or respect (neither did Hanna or McKinley).

Every man, be he capitalist, merchant, employer, laborer or professional man is
entitled to invest his capital, to carry on his business, to bestow his labor, or to exercise
his calling, if within the law according to his pleasure.
> —Moores and Co. vs. Bricklayers Union, reported January 20, 1890

As a judge Taft's most significant case was *Moores and Company v. Bricklayer's Union*, which involved a secondary boycott. Taft supported the organization of unions for collective bargaining and their right to strike. In his mind strikes became improper and illegal when the strikers boycotted an unrelated third party. Thus it was acceptable for workers to strike George Pullman and his railway car company, but it was improper and illegal for workers to strike railway companies for carrying Pullman cars. This punished companies and workers who were not parties to the dispute. This was not a popular view with labor unions who were struggling against powerful corporations and trusts. Taft, who worshipped the law, was a strong champion of individual rights.

In 1890 the opportunistic Foraker, running for office again, asked President Benjamin Harrison to appoint Taft to the U. S. Supreme Court. Harrison undoubtedly thought Taft, at 33, too young for that assignment and appointed him to the position of U. S. Solicitor General, the lawyer who argues the Federal position before the Supreme Court. As solicitor general Taft won fifteen of the seventeen cases he argued.

I have difficulty in holding the attention of the court. They seem to think when I begin to talk that there is a good chance to read all the letters that they have been waiting to read for some time, to eat lunch, and to devote their attention to correcting proofs, and other matters that have been delayed until my speech. However, I expect to gain a good deal of knowledge in addressing a lot of mummies and experience in not being overcome by circumstances.
—Letter to Father, June 16, 1890

I like judicial life and there is only one higher judicial position in the country than that....Federal judgeships like that just don't lie around loose, and if you don't get them when you can you will not get them when you would....It would keep me very poor, but I don't see that people with very modest incomes don't live as happily as those with fortunes.
—Letter to Father, March 1, 1891

Think of your going off on a trip with two Cabinet officers! If you get your heart's desire my darling it will put an end to all opportunities you now have of being thrown in with the bigwigs.
—Letter Nellie Taft to W. H. Taft, July 18, 1891

The Tafts had a different idea of his future. Will was easygoing and modest, a public figure who publicly and privately underestimated himself. Nellie was more aggressive. She thought destiny held great things for Will. She was also bored with lawyer talk, greatly preferring politics. Will, who had led a charmed life up to that point, knew how dirty politics could be, and he didn't want to get involved.

$\sim$

II. Federal Circuit Court Judge, 1892–1900; Professor and Dean of Law School, 1896–1900

Nationally the 1880s and 1890s were full of turmoil. It was a time of buccaneer capitalism and appalling labor conditions. In 1886 a dispute with the International Harvester company in Chicago led to the Haymarket riot, resulting in ten deaths. In 1892 the Homestead War broke out between Pinkerton detectives and Carnegie steel workers at Homestead, Pennsylvania, exacerbated by the attempted assassination of Henry Clay Frick, Carnegie's hard-line boss. The depression of 1893 led George Pullman to reduce wages for his workers in Pullman, Illinois. The railway workers under Eugene Victor Debs struck and tried to use a secondary boycott against the Pullman Company. No railway workers were to handle Pullman cars on any railroad anywhere in the country. To protect the U. S. Mail, President Grover Cleveland sent Federal troops to Chicago.

There were socialists, anarchists, and hard-line rightists who thought we were in a second civil war. Jacob Coxey of Massillon, Ohio, led a march of unemployed on Washington, demanding employment of workers on public works projects. Illinois's German-born governor, J. P. Altgeld (who had grown up in Mansfield, Ohio) caused a national ruckus by pardoning two of the Haymarket rioters. In 1896 William Jennings Bryan attributed all the problems of the country to the gold standard. McKinley won, but Bryan scared many.

Messers Bryan, Altgeld, Tillman, Debs, Coxey and the rest have not the power to rival the deeds of Marat, Barrere, Robespierre, but they are strikingly like the leaders of the Terror of France in mental and moral attitude.
—Theodore Roosevelt, October 1896

O, Hell. Go and live in Pullman and find out how much Pullman gets selling city water and gas ten percent higher to those damn fools. A man who doesn't meet his men halfway is a God damned fool.
    —Marc Hanna, 1894

Taft was critical of the Pullman strike by the American Railway Union because it involved an illegal secondary boycott. He had a local case involving the Toledo, Ann Arbor and North Michigan Railway, and eleven connecting railways. He found against the union and its secondary boycott. Another case was against Frank Phelan, a lieutenant of Debs, who had urged a secondary boycott against the bankrupt and federally supervised Cincinnati Southern Railway. In his decision against Phelan, Taft confirmed the right of labor to organize, bargain, and strike. He condemned the secondary boycott and the advocacy of violence.

His record on labor was not unmixed. In the *Voight* case, Voight, an employee, was forced to sign a waiver of liability for his employer. When he was seriously injured Taft ruled that such waivers were "oppressive, unreasonable, unjust and against public policy." (The U. S. Supreme Court reversed this decision; Congress changed the law in 1908 to make it consistent with Taft's decision.)

The *Narramore* case involved the doctrine of "assumed risk." Narramore, a brakeman, lost his leg when it became caught in an unprotected "frog" (junction). The railroad said Narramore knew about the junction and continued to work, therefore was ineligible for damages under the doctrine of "assumed risk." Taft thought that in this case the doctrine conflicted with railway safety legislation. Carefully writing a decision so as not to conflict with Ohio law he decided in favor of Narramore. This was a major labor case having influence on the entire country. Some leading businessmen were outraged, characterizing Taft as a radical western judge.

Finally in the *Addystone Pipe* case Taft brought life back to the Sherman Anti-Trust Act. After the Supreme Court had gutted it in the *American Sugar Refining* case in 1895, President Cleveland thought anti-trust action would have to take place at the state level. In *Addystone Pipe* Taft reversed a lower court ruling that had thrown out the Federal government's suit charging price fixing and profit sharing by six iron pipe companies in the Ohio and Mississippi valleys. The decision (like all of Taft's) was carefully written to prevent it from falling under the American Sugar case parameters. Taft found that the combination was clearly a direct restraint upon interstate commerce and an extensive scheme to control the whole commerce among thirty-six states in cast iron pipe. Therefore it was illegal. The decision gave new hope to future trustbusters like Theodore Roosevelt, Taft's future mentor, boss, friend, and ultimate political enemy.

~

III. Taft on the National Stage, 1900–1908

Always in my heart, the Philippine islands have had first place...
   —Speech, August 5, 1905

A. The Philippines 1900-1904

Now it is not well for the white man to hurry the Aryan brown, For the white man riles and the Aryan smiles, And it weareth the white man down.
   At the end of the fight is a tombstone white, with the name of the late deceased.
   And the epitaph drear, "a fool lies here" who tried to hustle the East.
   —Rudyard Kipling, *The Naulahka*, 1892

Taft was regarded by some as an outstanding judge. He thought he would be a judge the rest of his life, possibly on the Supreme Court. In January of 1900 he was beckoned to Washington by President McKinley. He was surprised by the offer to serve on a presidential commission to the Philippines. His integrity and cautious progressivism fit closely with that of McKinley. When Taft complained that he didn't know anything about the Philippines, didn't know Spanish, was against the war and Americans taking the Philippines, McKinley stated that he had been against the war and that since the U. S. had the Philippines it was its duty to give the Philippines the best government possible. He also said it was better to have an opponent of the war and the taking of the Philippines on the commission rather than the reverse. Secretary of War Elihu Root added that Taft had mostly served in the government since he was 21, that his country needed him now, and the only question was would he take the hard task? After talking with his brothers and the adventuresome Nellie, who always wanted to get Taft out of the judicial business, he accepted. Taft was to spend the next four years in the Philippines, first as commissioner then as governor-general. It was to dramatically change his life.

Taft's first problem in the Philippines was the military governor, General Arthur MacArthur. He had some of the *hauteur* later associated with his son,

General Douglas MacArthur. Symbolically, he sent a subordinate to greet Taft and the commission. As in many cases the military worldview was different from that of the civilians. The military did not mingle with the natives. Its approach was to conquer them and then worry about government.

Taft entered the islands with American idealism and his personal qualities of generosity and open friendliness. He mingled freely with the natives, treating them with respect, doing what would be later characterized as "winning their hearts and minds." He thought the military's arrogance and repression created its own opposition. MacArthur seemed to think the whole country opposed them, and he forecast the guerrilla war would last another ten years. The military undoubtedly thought that Taft and the other commissioners were a bunch of woolly-headed civilians. The clashes with MacArthur began immediately and were well-documented in letters from Taft to Secretary Root. Root, the supervisor of both, generally supported Taft. The civilian commission also had control of expenditures, giving it leverage in its bureaucratic battles with the military. The U. S. policies seemed to work, and many defected from Aguinaldo, the rebel leader. In 1901 Aguinaldo was captured and signed a loyalty oath to the constituted government. Taft became governor-general, and MacArthur was replaced by General A. R. Chaffee.

Taft aboard a water buffalo in the Philippines

*We hold the Philippines for the benefit of the Filipinos...We are not entitled to pass
a single act or to approve a single measure that has not that as its chief purpose.*
    —From a speech after Taft left the Philippines

Having won the bureaucratic battle with MacArthur, Taft tackled the major problems of the islands. The Philippines is a complicated place with 7,100 islands (730 inhabited) and many racial groups, religions, and languages. Like many colonies but especially those of the Spanish, the economic and political structure was controlled by a small elite. The elite were mostly Spanish or Spanish descended, with some Filipino mixture. There were also Roman Catholic friars who controlled over 400,000 of the best acres in the islands. The vast majority of the Filipinos were poor, landless, and uneducated. Those who had originally revolted attacked chiefly the friars and the elite.

The policies of McKinley and later Roosevelt, Root, and Taft were to set up a kind of peace corps to educate the populace, then the land would be bought from the Roman Catholic Church and turned over to the landless. Friars would be replaced with American priests, and the infrastructure would be improved with better roads, harbors, public health systems, and local government.

Taft viewed the American role in the Philippines as analogous to that of a court supervising an orphan. He was committed to the work. Twice he turned down Supreme Court appointments to continue to serve there. Once, the almost always healthy Taft nearly died of sepsis and had to return to the states. This led to the famous story, often told by Taft, that when he had returned to the Philippines he had traveled some twenty-five miles on a horse to a provincial town in the hills and still felt fine. He let Secretary Root know that. Root's question to the 300-pound Taft was, "How's the Horse?"

There were great difficulties during Taft's years in the Philippines: famines, typhoons, and a major outbreak of cholera. Some American administrators embezzled money, appalling Taft who prosecuted them with great vigor. He was also appalled at how some American businesses treated their potential Filipino customers.

*We have in these islands about eight thousand Americans and about eight millions
of Christian Filipinos. If business is to succeed here, it must be the sale of American goods to the
eight millions of Filipinos. One would think a child in business might understand that the worst
possible policy in attempting to sell goods is to abuse, berate and vilify your possible customers.*
    —Letter to H. C. Hollister, September 21, 1903

Taft's direct assignment to the Philippines ended in 1904 when Theodore Roosevelt asked him to replace the retiring Root as Secretary of War. Taft was again reluctant, but Roosevelt said he needed him and that Taft could continue to supervise the Philippines. Taft remained a supporter of the Philippines the rest of his life, beloved by many Filipinos.

B. Secretary of War 1904-1908

I have no particular aptitude for managing an army, nor do I know any thing about it.
   —Letter to Mrs. Bellamy Storer, October 26, 1903

Taft came home to be Secretary of War, counselor to the President, and a kind of special trouble shooter. He continued his involvement with the Philippines, sending requests to Congress for lower tariffs, currency reform, and infrastructure improvements. In 1905 he took a Congressional delegation to the Philippines (including Cincinnati Congressman Nicholas Longworth and his future wife, Alice Roosevelt, the President's daughter) in order to build political support for the Philippines.

On his way to the Philippines he made his third official visit to Japan. Japan had entered the world's stage as a major power. Taft and Roosevelt liked Japan. Taft considered the Japanese to be a hard working people with a government that genuinely cared about its people. The Roosevelt-Taft policy was to concede to the Japanese domination over Korea. They received assurances from the Japanese, the major power closest to the Philippines, that they would leave the Philippines alone. They also mediated the Russo-Japanese war, for which mediation Roosevelt received the Nobel Peace prize. There were domestic problems related to Japanese emigration in California. The "Yellow Peril" was used as a threatening term by the Hearst chain and other irresponsible newspapers. San Francisco tried to deny education to Japanese children. Roosevelt and Taft had difficulty in controlling the local situation, but the Japanese government secretly agreed to slow down emigration.

In one of his high-handed acts President Roosevelt had supported the independence of Panama, a province of Colombia, and blocked Colombia's attempted recovery of it. The purpose was to find a better negotiating partner for the construction of the Panama canal. Taft was given the job of pointing out to the Panamanians the advantages of the canal, which mostly involved the massive expenditures of American money in the local economy. The construction process

was going very slowly and when the chief engineering officer resigned, Taft recommended Colonel George W. Goethals, one of the heroes of the canal construction.

In 1906 the U. S. got more deeply involved in Cuba. McKinley had wanted the Cubans to be independent. Congress passed the Platt Amendment, which allowed U. S. intervention in Cuban affairs. There was a disputed election and a threat of rebellion. Roosevelt sent Taft, who served as a provisional administrator. He saw his role as a temporary receiver who would reorganize things for the long term.

Incidentally Taft is a cabinet officer. Primarily he is a proconsul of good faith to fractious islands; an ambassador to fractious islands at four corners of the earth.
—Frederick Palmer, *Colliers Weekly,* April 13, 1907

Taft made one severe error as Secretary of War. In Brownsville, Texas, there had been a riot involving some black soldiers and a white bartender had been killed. When Roosevelt could not find the guilty party he ordered 160 black soldiers, including six medal of honor winners, discharged. The judicious Taft appealed to Roosevelt to hold a court of inquiry, but Roosevelt, who thought he knew much more about the army than Taft, refused. Taft against his better judgment went along with Roosevelt.

~

IV. Taft as President, 1909–1913

I would never run for President if you guaranteed the office. It is awful to be made afraid of one's shadow.
—Taft, March 31, 1904

In 1908 Taft was Theodore Roosevelt's candidate for President. He defeated William Jennings Bryan in Bryan's third try for the presidency. Taft was inaugurated on one of the coldest days in Washington's history. "I always said it would be a cold day in hell when I got to be President," he joked to a worried Nellie.

Taft became President with several major disadvantages. The Republicans had been in office for a long time and seemed to have both the arrogance and

◀ *Taft at full figure*

149

complacency brought about by such tenure. The party was splitting between progressives and conservatives. Teddy Roosevelt, a master of playing to the crowd, had kept the party together during his nearly two terms in office. He had supported Taft for the Presidency, but any President who was not Teddy Roosevelt was unlikely to please Teddy Roosevelt very long.

The Tafts were one of those couples where weaknesses in one were offset by strengths in the other. He tended to be open, trusting, and uncalculating, although when he was serious, he was a little stodgy. Nellie, a musician, liked adventure. She was ambitious, clever, skeptical, and relished the game of politics. Early in his term, Nellie had a near-fatal stroke that left her, for a time, speechless, and thus Taft had to operate without his chief political advisor. This loss was incalculable.

Taft took his campaign promises seriously, as though they were contracts with the people. The clever Roosevelt, like most politicians, ignored or modified his own pledges. The seriousness with which Taft made his promises would cause him difficulties throughout his presidency.

Taft's first political problem began with the issue of "Uncle" Joe Cannon, Republican leader of the House of Representatives. George W. Norris (born Sandusky County, Ohio) and other progressives asked Taft to join them in over-

Taft: a family of connections

throwing Cannon. Cannon was dictatorial, obnoxious, and unpleasant. Taft probably would have liked to get rid of Cannon, but that would have most likely brought chaos upon the House. To get his program passed Taft needed Cannon the same way that Benjamin Harrison and William McKinley needed "Czar" Reed. Taft's failure to come out against Cannon began the erosion of support.

The next issue was tariff reform, an issue the astute Roosevelt had refused to touch. In 1909 the country was running a deficit of $100 million and there were problems of trusts abusing their positions. Taft thought tariff reform could help solve both. He proposed to the House a bill mostly reducing tariffs, which was largely accepted. In the Senate, however, Republicans led by Nelson Aldrich and Henry Cabot Lodge, gutted the House bill. Most tariffs remained high although Taft was able to obtain a few reforms: reciprocity, a one percent tax on corporations, and most important in Taft's mind, a new tariff commission, which Taft thought could look objectively at the entire system. Against the urgings of many Taft signed the bill. It was a moderate reform but based upon the original hope— or even the House bill— another political loss.

Perhaps Taft's biggest political problems related to conservation. Roosevelt became a hero to conservationists by stretching the Antiquities Act to set aside the Grand Canyon, Mount Olympus, and other unique sites as national monuments. But his record wasn't spotless. Roosevelt's interior secretary, James R. Garfield (son of President Garfield), in consultation with the head of the forest service, Gifford Pinchot, authorized a dam in the Hetch Hetchy area of Yosemite, which resulted ultimately in splitting that area out of Yosemite. This was not the first or the last, but the most serious assault on a national park ever.

Taft the lawyer questioned actions taken by the non-lawyer Roosevelt in setting aside land by executive order rather than law. His point was that what could be set aside by executive order could also be canceled by executive order. He replaced Garfield with Richard Ballinger, a former commissioner of public lands under Roosevelt. Almost immediately Ballinger got involved in disputes with Pinchot. Taft supported Ballinger and fired Pinchot. This cost him political support and undoubtedly opened a rift with Roosevelt. Ballinger retired because of sickness and Taft's second Interior Secretary, Walter L. Fisher, was very effective. He became an advocate for a national parks service to preserve and protect the parks. This goal was achieved in 1916 under the Wilson administration. Glacier National Park also came into being under the Taft administration.

Taft had genuine achievements as President. His Attorney General, George W. Wickersham, completed anti-trust cases against John D. Rockefeller's Standard Oil and James B. Duke's American Tobacco Companies. He also initiated a case against U. S. Steel that offended, among others, Theodore Roosevelt, who was mentioned in the legal papers filed in the suit. Altogether the Taft administration initiated more than twice as many anti-trust cases in its four years than the Roosevelt administration did in its seven and one-half years.

Taft ran the government like a corporate executive. He relied on cabinet members to run their own departments. As a part of this process he was the first President to ask cabinet members for their department budgets. Ultimately this resulted in major budget reforms for the Federal government in the 1920s and illustrates Taft's objective way of managing the government.

Taft successfully proposed reforms of the Interstate Commerce Commission, including the creation of a commerce court. He had a National Children's Bureau established, and named Julia Clifford Lathrop to head it, the first female bureau head in the Federal government. He requested that campaign financial contributions and expenditures be made public. He expanded the merit system in the foreign service, and finally he had a postal savings system created to protect the money of the small saver. One idea he proposed that was unsuccessful was the national chartering of corporations, a radical idea even today.

In foreign affairs, he became famous for "Dollar Diplomacy." His idea was that dollar diplomacy was an extension of the Monroe Doctrine and that the United States would seek to influence other nations, not by force of arms but by investments in their economies. Up to that time of his presidency Taft had been the most widely traveled President in history. He, like McKinley, thought international trade and investment were positive and should be encouraged by the government. Like Benjamin Harrison, he thought disputes could be objectively arbitrated. His Secretary of State, Philander C. Knox (a graduate of Alliance College), negotiated arbitration treaties with Great Britain and France. He also negotiated freer trade with Canada, but the treaty was rejected by the Canadians.

Despite his achievements Taft was bitterly criticized by the newspapers. He was not an exciting or dramatic speaker, his family wasn't entertaining like that of the Roosevelts, and he retained his essential modesty. He was also the first Presidential golfer. He liked golf and he admitted it, which brought him a barrage of criticism.

In 1910 Teddy Roosevelt returned from Africa and Europe. From then on, Taft's days as President were numbered. He won the Republican nomination in 1912. Teddy protested by starting his own party, the Bull Moose party. Woodrow Wilson (father from Steubenville, Ohio, mother from Chillicothe, Ohio) was the Democratic nominee. He beat the split Republicans, taking forty-one per cent of the popular vote. Roosevelt came in second and Taft was a distant third. Taft was disappointed but soon became his old self: when he met someone who said they voted for him he said, "You are of a small but distinct minority in whose opinions I heartily concur."

153

V. Law Professor, 1913–1921

I think the whole country admires you, as I do, the generous spirit in which you have sunk all considerations of party and have come to my support at this critical juncture in our history. You may be sure that the suggestions you make have great weight with me, and will constitute part of my serious thought at this time of perplexity....

—President Woodrow Wilson to W. H. Taft after the sinking of the Luisitania, 1915

After leaving the presidency Taft was a law professor at Yale. He also wrote articles and traveled around the country speaking. Although he did not particularly like Woodrow Wilson, he supported his efforts to keep the country out of World War I. After the United States became involved in the War in 1917 Wilson appointed Taft to the National War Labor Board. (Theodore Roosevelt's fate was different. He thought that the United States should immediately be involved in the war and criticized Wilson for his "pussyfooting." Wilson got even by denying Roosevelt a combat role when the United States became involved in the war). After the war Taft supported Wilson's treaty on the League of Nations, which was killed by Henry Cabot Lodge and the U. S. Senate.

VI. Supreme Court Justice, 1921–1930

In 1921 President Warren G. Harding appointed Taft Chief Justice of the Supreme Court, a position Taft had long desired. At the time, all Federal courts were overwhelmed with work, much of it resulting from Prohibition. Taft, lobbying Congress, obtained a number of reforms, including the creation of new Federal courts, added judges, and procedures for the Supreme Court to better control its own docket. He also wanted standardized procedures for Federal courts but was blocked by one senator. Finally he got authorization for a new Supreme Court building. This was both practical and symbolic. The court needed space and it needed visibility as a co-equal branch of government. Altogether, Taft is regarded as a great court strategist and administrator.

His role on the development of law is more controversial. Taft thought individual property rights were fundamental. For this he was classified as a conservative. In the context of his own life this approach made sense. He grew up in a happy, achieving family. He was a generous and considerate man. He wanted everyone to have the advantages that he had and saw these advantages accruing from individual liberty. He thought this freedom needed to be protected from encroachments by large institutions, especially governments, and that was what courts were for. What distinguished Taft from other conservatives was his concern for the little man. One of the main impetuses for his court reforms was to make justice more accessible, less costly, and more certain than it had been.

Taft served with three great justices who sometimes dissented from his opinions: Oliver Wendell Holmes, Louis D. Brandeis, and later Harlan Fiske Stone. In general they believed that property rights were less absolute, and the law needed to grow with the times. Holmes, whose father was a poet, and Brandeis both had the ability to write memorable thoughts and concepts into their decisions, Holmes: "Taxes are what we pay for civilized society," "...the best test of truth is the power of the thought to get itself accepted in the competition of the market," and "The most stringent protection of free speech would not protect a man in falsely shouting fire in a theater and causing a panic...." Brandeis: "...a single courageous state may...serve as a laboratory and try novel social economic experiments" and "The greatest dangers to liberty lurk in insidious encroachment by men of zeal, well-meaning, but without understanding." Taft himself was not a good phrasemaker. Perhaps his experience suited him better for administration. He brought industry, humor, and management to the Court. In 1924 Taft had a heart attack. There is evidence that in 1927-28 he slowed down and became less effective. He retired from the Court on February 3, 1930.

We call you Chief Justice still, for we cannot give up the title by which we have known you for all these later years and which you have made so dear to us. We cannot let you leave us without trying to tell you how dear you have made it. You have come to us from achievement in other fields, and with the prestige of the illustrious place you lately had held, and you showed in a new form your voluminous capacity for work and for getting work done, your humor that smoothed the rough places, your golden heart that has brought you love from every side, and most of all from your brethren whose tasks you have made happy and light....

—From the Justices of the Supreme Court upon learning of Taft's resignation

●Deaths

Taft died at age 72, March 8, 1930. He had arteriosclerosis. Nellie Taft died May 22, 1943. She lived long enough to see her son, Senator Robert A. Taft, become a serious candidate for nomination as President.

Its great to be great, but greater to be human. He was our great human fellow, because there was more of him to be human. We are parting with 300 pounds of solid charity to everybody, and love and affection for all his fellow men.
—Will Rogers

●Visiting Taft Sites

William Howard and Nellie Taft are buried in Arlington National Cemetery, across the river from Washington, DC. The Tafts had a positive impact on Washington: Nellie Taft arranged for the planting of the Japanese cherry trees, which are beautiful in the spring; William Howard oversaw construction of the Lincoln Memorial and the Supreme Court building.

In Cincinnati the Taft home is located at 2038 Auburn Avenue, on one of the seven hills of Cincinnati. Four of its rooms are decorated as they would have been in Will's years there. Upstairs is a small museum. The Taft Museum, once home of Will's half brother, and financial supporter, Charles Phelps Taft, and sister-in-law, Anne Sinton Taft, is located near the site of the old Fort Washington, at 316 Pike Street. It is a beautiful house on a nice square. It contains murals by Robert S. Duncanson, pre-Civil War free black who achieved some national fame as an artist. Have a map in hand or ask for specific directions as it is hard to reach because of freeways and one-way streets.

●Works Relevant to Understanding the Tafts

A. Biographical

➻Anderson, Donald F. 1973. *William Howard Taft.* Ithaca, NY: Cornell University Press.

Although not a complete biography like Pringle's (see below) Anderson had

William Howard Taft National Historic Site, Cincinnati, Ohio

access to material that was unavailable to Pringle. This book explains the context of decisions that Taft made. In that way it is fairer than any other book on Taft. Although there may be some implicit irony, the book generally contrasts Taft unfavorably with that great master of public relations, Teddy Roosevelt.

Anderson, Judith Icke. 1981. *William Howard Taft: An Intimate History.* New York: Norton.

This is psychohistory, which looks at everything from a particular viewpoint. What I don't like about psychohistory is that it turns virtues like loyalty and honesty into pathologies (usually blamed on the parents) and often stretches interpretations to fit preconceived ideas. This book provides certain insights but in my view goes too far.

Mason, Alpheus Thomas. 1964. *William Howard Taft, Chief Justice.* New York: Simon and Schuster.

Mason was a prolific writer on the Supreme Court and law, including biographies of Justices Brandeis and Harlan Fiske Stone. The book contains separate essays on Taft's legal and Supreme Court life. I don't think Mason fully appreciated Taft's early life and views. However his conclusion that Taft was a great architect of the Court and had a rare ability to harmonize a diverse and often strong-willed group of individuals seems precisely right.

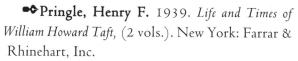

Pringle, Henry F. 1939. *Life and Times of William Howard Taft,* (2 vols.). New York: Farrar & Rhinehart, Inc.

These are excellent books based upon the voluminous records and letters of the Taft family. Pringle, a biographer of Theodore Roosevelt, is very perceptive about both men.

Ross, Ishbel. 1964. *An American Family: The Tafts 1678-1964.* Cleveland, OH: The World Publishing Co.

William Howard Taft was first, last, and always, a family man. This book shows how one generation pushes, inspires, and supports the next. It begins with Alphonso Taft; his first wife Fanny Phelps, who died tragically at age 29; their two children; and his second wife, Louisa Torrey, and their three sons (including William Howard) and one daughter. The Tafts, Phelpses, and the Torreys were literate, well-read people who wrote thousands of letters providing great insight on personal and political issues. The book devotes chapters to William Howard and Nellie's children: Senator Robert A. Taft (Mr. Republican of the 1940's and 50's), Charles Phelps Taft (II), and Helen Herron Taft Manning.

Taft: "The nearer I get to the inauguration of my successor, the greater relief I feel."

∾Taft, Mrs. William Howard (Helen or Nellie). 1914. *Recollections of Full Years.* New York: Dodd, Mead and Co.

This is the first memoir published by a first lady. (Julia Dent Grant's was written earlier but published later.) Mrs. Taft shows herself to be smart and aggressive, a great adventure seeker. She was also the family worrier. Despite her husband's often breathtaking responsibilities he seemed to meet every situation with equanimity and humor; she worried. Implicit in all this is a generally smoothly functioning team, looking at situations quite differently but listening to each other. The Tafts were world travelers, and we owe to Mrs. Taft's idea for cherry trees in Washington to her visits to Japan.

B. Non-biographical

●Dixon, W. MacNeile and Grierson, H. J. C., editors. 1909. *The English Parnassus.* London: Oxford University Press.

This book contains two of the works read at William Howard Taft's funeral: *Character of the Happy Warrior* by William Wordsworth (1806) and *Ode on the Death of the Duke of Wellington* (1852) by Alfred Lord Tennyson.

●McCullough, David. 1977. *The Path Between the Seas: The Creation of the Panama Canal, 1970-1914.* New York: A Touchstone book, Simon and Schuster.

This is a prize-winning book that tells the dramatic story of the building of the Panama Canal. It has a large section on the valiant but unsuccessful French effort. It describes the interactions of many vivid characters, giving appropriate credit to key players like Ferdinand de Lesseps, Teddy Roosevelt, Phillipe Bunau-Varilla, George Goethals, and William Gorgas. Taft was a key player in picking Goethals and overseeing much of the effort. Grant deserves some credit for ordering the initial surveys of Central America for a canal. Steamshovels used in digging the Panama Canal were built in Marion and Bucyrus, Ohio.

●Tarbell, Ida M. *History of the Standard Oil Company,* (2 Vols.). 1904 (Republished in 1966). New York: McClure, Phillips & Co.

This is justifiably a classic. It tells the story of how John Davison Rockefeller and a few of his associates, including Henry M. Flagler, Steven Harkness, and others turned Cleveland into the oil capital of the world. Rockefeller, a quiet man, often working behind the scenes, had astonishing talent. He was a good numbers man who thought strategically. He surrounded himself with brilliant people of all types and was ruthless and relentless. He manipulated the railroads through rebates and drawbacks. He started his domination with refiners in Cleveland (later in Pittsburgh, Philadelphia, New York, and Baltimore), and soon dominated producers in northwest Pennsylvania and later pipelines and marketers. The Standard Oil Trust at one time dominated eighty per cent of the U. S. market. The Standard Oil Trust created many enemies resulting in lawsuits, investigations by state legislatures and Congress, and ultimately its break-up under the Sherman Anti-Trust Act, initiated under Theodore Roosevelt and completed under William Howard Taft.

●**Tuchman, Barbara W.** 1966. *The Proud Tower: a Portrait of the World Before the War 1890-1914.* New York: The Macmillan Company.

This is a kind of prequel to *The Guns of August.* It shows a world that the United States was increasingly involved with, culminating in the United States participation in World War I. It covers political developments in England, France, and Germany and how those countries tried to cope with industrialization and some kind of balance between the rich and the poor. It also has sections on anarchism, socialism, and a special section on how Congressman Tom Reed of Maine became "Czar" Reed. The most dramatic section in the book is on the Dreyfus case in France where paranoia, lies, coverups, and anti-Semitism created a huge national and, to some extent, international scandal.

●**White, William Allen.** 1946. *Autobiography.* New York: The Macmillan Company.

White was the editor of the *Emporia Gazette,* a small town paper in Kansas, and a prodigious writer. He met and talked with Presidents Benjamin Harrison, Cleveland, McKinley, Taft, Wilson, Harding, and Hoover as well as non-Presidents like Marc Hanna, William Jennings Bryan, and Robert LaFollette. He became a close personal friend of Theodore Roosevelt whom he admired greatly. Recognizing both strengths and weaknesses in humanity, he has candid appraisals of all. With McKinley he was frustrated that he could not penetrate his reserve. Under the Roosevelt influence he is probably unfair to both Taft and Wilson. Journalists supposedly write the "rough drafts of history" but unfortunately many of White's sometimes superficial views seem to have gotten far beyond the rough draft stage.

Warren Gameliel Harding
Small City Publisher as President

29th President
March 4, 1921-August 2, 1923

Warren G. Harding was considered amiable and handsome, an empty suit manipulated by others all the way from small town publisher to the White House. There, he was considered to have run an out-of-control administration. Some historians said he was our worst President. Three self-serving associates came out with books after he died. One accused him of being a philanderer, another a puppet, still another claimed he was poisoned by his own wife. His papers, which might have provided some defense, were not available for more than forty years after he died. His reputation was established by scandal-mongers and journalists. It is likely he was a philanderer, like several other twentieth century Presidents. It is unlikely that he was murdered, and he was not a puppet. He was a man of limited education and interests but also a talented businessman and clever politician with a self-deprecating style that often caused people to underestimate him. Warren G. Harding was in many ways the average man as President, and like any average man he had his strengths and he had his weaknesses.

◀ *Harding: the average man as President*

Boys flying kites haul in their white winged birds;
You can't do that when you're flying words.
"Careful with fire" is good advice we know;
"Careful with words" is ten times doubly so.
Thoughts unexpressed may sometimes fall back dead;
But God himself can't kill them when they're said.

——A favorite poem of Harding's by Will Carleton, Midwest poet

●**Family Heritage:** Harding was born November 2, 1865, in Blooming Grove (Corsica), Ohio. Harding was the first President born after the Civil War. Harding's family was English, Scots, Irish, and Dutch. There were rumors that he had Negro blood. Harding himself was unsure but an issue was made of it all his life. Harding's father, George Tryon Harding, also born in Blooming Grove, was a fifer and drummer in the Civil War. George Tryon Harding was a restless individual who never achieved financial stability. He taught school for a while and then became a doctor. He outlived his son, the first President's father to do so. Warren's mother, Phoebe Dickerson Harding, was a midwife who also became a doctor, and Warren was the oldest of six surviving children. All his life Warren looked after his parents and to some extent, his siblings.

●**Religion:** Harding's father was a Baptist. His mother was a Methodist who became a Seventh Day Adventist. Harding was nominally a Baptist. Towards the end of his life he reported a "conscious spiritual influence" on his actions.

The Duchess: "I have only one real hobby——my husband."

164

●**Education:** Harding graduated from Ohio Central College, Iberia, Ohio. He liked speaking and writing, founded the campus newspaper, and played the alto cornet. Beyond the daily paper, Harding had little interest in reading.

●**Wife:** Harding married Florence Kling De Wolfe, an unattractive divorcee with a young son. Florence was the daughter of a successful, strong-willed businessman in Marion, Ohio. She was just as strong-willed. She was a graduate of the Cincinnati Conservatory of Music where she majored in piano. Her father disowned her after she married Pete De Wolfe, an alcoholic from a well-to-do Marion family. To support herself and her son, she borrowed a piano and began giving music lessons. Later she developed a chronic kidney ailment. She and Warren had no children. Warren was probably the father of Elizabeth Ann Christian, an illegitimate daughter by Nan Britton. He also had an affair with Carrie Phillips, wife of a Marion department store owner.

Never let a husband travel alone.
—Florence Kling Harding, the "Duchess"

●**Personal Characteristics:** Harding was easygoing, likable, and friendly. He was a naturally sympathetic "people person" who enjoyed doing small favors. In politics he generally felt much stronger about people than issues. He usually followed the party line without antagonizing his opponents. He was a good poker player and this showed in his political strategy, waiting his turn, never overly aggressive. He was restless and loved to travel. His health was often problematic. Five times he went to Dr. Kellogg's sanitarium in Battle Creek, Michigan. It is likely that in his forties he developed arteriosclerosis and high blood pressure.

Warren it's a good thing you wasn't born a gal.

Why?

Because you'd always be in the family way all the time. You can't say no.
—Warren G. Harding's father, and young Warren, as told
to the National Press Club by Warren G. Harding, 1922

I. Early Life 1865-1884

Warren grew up in Caledonia, Ohio. He was popular, liked to perform by playing the cornet, later by speaking, and worked part-time as a printer's devil for the *Caledonia Argus*. At college he was mainly interested in debate and speech.

II. Editor–Publisher, 1884–1920

WE HAVE PURCHASED THE STAR AND WE WILL STAY
—Headline, *Marion Star, November 26, 1884*

...He plays the lickspittle to a class of men who like such practices. Then he swells up believing that no good can be done without his sanction and advice, he foams at the mouth whenever his sordid mind grasps anything done politically without his counsel; and he rolls his eyes and straightaway evolves from his inner consciousness a double-twisted, unadulterated, canvas-backed lie that would make the devil blush. His sordid soul is gangrened with jealousy...
—Editorial about George Gordon Bennett Crawford, rival Republican editor and publisher, in March 1886, after Crawford insulted Harding's father

Star is Rats spelled backward.
—One of Crawford's insults in the Spring of 1886

Edgewood Hub is in the register as a mark of his breeding, but to us just Hub, a little Boston terrier, whose sentinennt (sic) *eye mirrored the fidelity and devotion of his loyal heart. The veterinarian said he was poisoned; perhaps he was—his mute sufferings suggested it. One is reluctant to believe that a human being that claims man's estate could be so hateful a coward as to ruthlessly torture and kill a trusting victim, made defenceless through his confidence in the human master, but there are such. One honest look from Hub's trusting eyes were worth a hundred lying greetings from such inhuman beings, though they wore the habiliment of men.*
—Article in *Marion Star*, March 11, 1913

Harding found his niche as editor-publisher of *The Marion Star*. He wrote passably and like many of his generation loved alliteration and the coining of new words like "normalcy." He often wrote with low-key humor. He took a marginal weekly paper and in the face of fierce competition turned it into a successful daily. He sold advertising, wrote articles and editorials, and sometimes did the printing. He treated his employees decently, never firing anybody, and created a stock company that was one of the first in America to give employees ownership shares. After the paper was well established, and during one of Warren's trips to Dr. Kellogg's, Duchess took over as circulation manager. Like many strong-willed people she gave the appearance of being in charge. One of their paperboys was Norman Thomas, six-time Socialist candidate for President. He had great affection for both Hardings but especially Warren.

After the paper became a going concern Harding hired competent writers and managers. He liked to socialize, to write editorials, and make speeches ("bloviate," in his terminology). He was a natural for politics and in 1892 agreed to run for auditor as a sacrificial lamb in heavily Democratic Marion County.

~

III. Harding in State and National Politics, 1899-1921

I suppose you want to be President some day. Every Ohio youngster does. Well, you better keep closer in touch with us fellows in Cleveland and not train so exclusively with those damn troublemakers in Cincinnati.
        —Marc Hanna early in Harding's political career.

Harding was cut off from politics in Marion by the domination of the old guard Republicans led by his father-in-law, Amos Kling. It was futile to run in the county because it was Democratic. Harding decided to go around them by running for state senator from the 13th district, composed of Logan, Hardin, Union, and Marion counties. Under the system then in place it was Marion County's turn to nominate the candidate. Harding skillfully outmaneuvered the old guard Republicans of Marion, got the nomination, and thanks to heavily Republican Logan and Union Counties, won the election.

As a noted "harmonizer" in the senate he followed the party line and became popular with members of both parties. He introduced a measure to reform municipal government, which de-emphasized politics in local elections, created local civil services and municipal ownership of certain utilities. He got the measure passed and left town. While he was gone, it was reconsidered and rejected.

Harding was a party regular and a compromise candidate for the Presidency, running against another Ohioan.

In the next election he broke precedent by asking to be renominated. He was and returned to the state senate where he was elected senate leader. There, he became friends with Nicholas Longworth, a Cincinnati political figure (and future son-in-law of Theodore Roosevelt). During this term Harding was asked to renominate "Fire Alarm" Joe Foraker for reelection to the U. S. Senate. This was an honor but also entailed some risk in Ohio's three-cornered political system (Marc Hanna of Cleveland, Boss Cox of Cincinnati, and Foraker).

During this term the Ohio Supreme Court threw out the "ripper" system of state legislature rule over the cities. Therefore the state had to establish a new system. Harding "harmonized" between the reformers and the bosses, and a new law was passed that met the court's requirements and was acceptable to the legislature. In 1902 Harding wanted to run for governor of Ohio. Myron Herrick, a successful businessman and close friend of the late William McKinley, also wanted to run. In the end, Hanna supported Herrick as the best antidote to reform mayors Tom Johnson of Cleveland and Samuel "Golden Rule" Jones of Toledo. Harding was given the lieutenant governorship as consolation prize. The Republican slogan that year was "Hanna, Herrick, Harding and Harmony." As governor, Herrick offended too many groups (especially members of the Anti-Saloon League after vetoing a bill they wrote). Harding knew Herrick was finished politically even though Herrick intended to run in 1904. Harding, not wishing an association with Herrick's ticket, announced he would not run for a second term as lieutenant governor. Herrick was badly defeated by John M. Pattison of Clermont County. Ironically, Pattison died soon after the election and the Republican lieutenant governor, Andrew Harris of Eaton, became governor.

After his political retirement Harding wrote articles and made speeches for various Republican candidates and spoke on the Chatauqua circuit. In 1910 Harding was nominated for governor but lost badly to Judson Harmon, a former Attorney General in the second Grover Cleveland administration. In 1912 the Republican party was in chaos. Harry Daugherty, a marginal politician and political fixer from Washington Court House took over as state chairman. When the Progressives split the Republican party in Ohio, Harding stuck with Taft. He was rewarded by being given the assignment of nominating Taft at the Republican convention. He came out for "progression."

Progression is not proclamation nor palaver. It is not pretense nor play on prejudice.
It is not personal pronouns nor perennial pronouncement. It is not the perturbation of a people
passion-wrought, nor a promise proposed. Progression is everlastingly lifting the standards that
marked the end of the world's march yesterday and planting them on new and advanced heights
today. Tested by such a standard, President Taft is the greatest progressive of our age.
    —Harding speech nominating Taft, June 20, 1912

Harding's introduction to the national stage was not harmonious. The Roosevelt delegates, who thought Taft had stolen the nomination from Roosevelt, disrupted the speech. Still, Harding earned points with the Republican regulars who, despite the turmoil with the Progressives, would maintain party control in Ohio. Wilson won the presidency and James M. Cox, a Dayton newspaperman, was elected Governor of Ohio.

(Wilson) is a clean, learned, honorable patriotic man, and the country had better risk
the dangers of the economic policy for which his party stands than return to power "the great
personality" (Teddy Roosevelt) insane with ambition, heedless of tradition or the lessons
of history....
    —*Star* editorial after the 1912 election

The year 1914 brought the first direct election of U. S. senators. Senator Theodore Burton, a Cleveland intellectual, withdrew. "Fire Alarm" Joe Foraker was ready to go, but he had charges against him that from his previous term in office that he was on the payroll of Standard Oil. Marc Hanna's son, Dan, blocked Foraker. Harding became the party's compromise choice for senator. In the Republican primary he defeated Foraker and Congressman Ralph Cole. Frank Willis, of Delaware, Ohio, was nominated as governor. The Democrats renominated Cox for governor and nominated Timothy S. Hogan, an Irish Catholic, to run against Harding. Hogan had put a number of crooked state officials in jail when he was state attorney general. The Progressives put up James R. Garfield, son of the former President, for governor and Arthur Garford, an Elyria bicycle seat manufacturer, as senator. Harding and Willis won, and it looked like the Republican party was strong again.

The first session of the new Congress began in December of 1915. Harding established a mediocre record as a senator. He generally voted with his party but missed roll call votes 43% of the time. He did better socially, making friends in both parties, including Democrats Franklin D. Roosevelt, Josephus Daniels, and Newton Baker. He and the Duchess made friends with Ned and Evalyn Walsh McLean, two rich and spoiled young adults. Ned inherited *The Cincinnati Enquirer* and *The Washington Post.* Evalyn's father had struck it rich after prospecting for twenty years in Colorado. Evalyn bought the Star of India and the Hope diamonds, and because of a series of misfortunes in her family the Hope diamond is considered bad luck.

I think you know me as well as anybody in Ohio, and you know I am unsuited to the higher position if it were possible for me to attain it, and you know I am truthful when I say that I do not desire it...
—Letter to Malcom Jennings about the presidency, April 1916

In 1916, World War I was the big issue. Harding, Herrick, Burton, and Willis were all mentioned as dark horse candidates for the Presidency. Harding was given the honor of making the keynote speech at the Republican convention, and he bombed. Charles Evans Hughes was nominated by the Republicans. Woodrow Wilson ran on the slogan, "He kept us out of war!" The election was extremely close, with Wilson ultimately carrying both California and Ohio, the loss of either one of which would have cost him the presidency.

In December of 1916 Wilson tried and almost got a negotiated "peace without victory." In April of 1917 the United States joined the war. Teddy Roosevelt, who had called Wilson a "pussy footer" for not entering the war in 1914, immediately offered to lead volunteers. Wilson, who had a long memory and who could be vindictive, kept Teddy and the army's top general, Leonard Wood, at home. After some initial blundering, U. S. forces helped turn the tide and an armistice was declared in 1918 at 11 a.m. on the eleventh day of the eleventh month. The war was over, but its impact lived on in countless ways. Quentin Roosevelt, Theodore's youngest son, was killed in an air battle in July of 1918. It dispirited Teddy. He told his biographer, "I would not lift a finger to get the nomination. Since Quentin's death the world seems to have shut down on me." Roosevelt, the favorite for the Republican nomination in 1920, died suddenly on January 6, 1919.

At the beginning of the second half of his second term, Woodrow Wilson seemed to have everything under control. He was a hero in Europe, as well as the United States, for his conduct during "the war to end all wars" and "to make the world safe for democracy." He went to Europe (against some advice) with his "14 points," a preconceived plan for peace. He achieved some goals but did not greatly change the French, who wanted to punish the Germans, and the British, who wanted to maintain their empire. He offended the Irish, the Italians, and a group to be heard from in the future, the Vietnamese. He returned to the United States slightly tarnished. There Senators Henry Cabot Lodge, Warren G. Harding, and others were waiting for him.

Wilson was determined that he would defeat Senate opposition to the League of Nations. He embarked on a trip to take his cause to the people. While on this trip, he suffered a near fatal stroke. He would never be the same.

There was a lot of turmoil after the war: strikes, race riots, bombings, and threats of Bolshevism. Industry cut back, many soldiers returned to unemployment, and farm prices fell. The official policy of the newly created Federal Reserve was deflation. Many yearned for simplicity, "normalcy" in Harding's terminology.

For the Republicans, Theodore Roosevelt's death created a vacuum. The leading contender for President was Teddy's old commander and former top general in the army, Leonard Wood. Wood, a morally upright man, had a long history of distinguished service. If Wilson had allowed him to lead the American forces in Europe, he probably would have been elected President in 1920. Another candidate was Frank Lowden, reform governor of Illinois and son-in-law of George Pullman, famed for the Pullman strike in 1894. Herbert Hoover, a millionaire businessman who had given up business for public service, emerged from the war as a national hero for feeding starving Europeans. He was non-political though; no one knew if he was a Republican or a Democrat. There was also Hiram Johnson of California, a former progressive, who didn't support Taft in 1912 or Hughes in 1916. Harding entered the race as a "favorite son," probably to protect his senate seat. Harry Daugherty became his manager. Daugherty, who had never been respected but always survived, defined and executed a strategy remarkably similar to that of Hayes, Garfield, and Benjamin Harrison, making Harding second, third, or fourth choice of many delegates.

> *I do not cry over spilled milk in politics or business ventures; I follow the plan of looking out for a fresh cow in some new pasture.*
> —Letter from Harry Daugherty to Harding, December 30, 1918

Harding: *Am I a big enough man for the race?*

Daugherty: *Don't make me laugh! The days of giants in the Presidential chair is passed. Our so-called Great Presidents were all made by the conditions of war under which they dominated the office. Greatness in the Presidential chair is largely an illusion of the people.*
> —Conversation: Harding and Daugherty in 1919

> *I haven't a ghost of a chance for the presidency.*
> —To Harry M. Daugherty, June 1920

It happened again. The leaders blocked each other and Harding, called by a fellow senator, "the best of the second raters," won the nomination. For Vice President the party named the hero of the Boston police strike, Calvin Coolidge. In November, Harding ran against the other Ohio newspaperman, James M. Cox, with future leader Franklin D. Roosevelt as his Vice President nominee. The Socialists nominated their jailed leader, Eugene Victor Debs. With the nation-wide support of the Anti-Saloon League and the desire to return to "normalcy," Harding won easily. It was an especial triumph for Daugherty, who had finally earned respect.

The President liked to play golf twice a week. ▶

IV. President, 1921–1923

*Our most dangerous tendency is to expect too much of government, and at the same time
do for it too little....*

*...not heroism but healing, not nostrums but normalcy, not revolution but restoration, not
agitation but adjustment, not surgery but serenity, not the dramatic but the dispassionate, not
experiment but equipoise, not submergence in internationality but sustainment in triumphant
nationality.*
    —From Harding Inaugural Address, March 4, 1921

A. Some Positives

*Here in the United States we are but freshly turned from the burial of an unknown
American soldier, when a nation sorrowed while paying him tribute. Whether it was spoken or
not, a hundred millions of our people were summarizing the inexcusable causes, the incalculable
cost, the unspeakable sacrifices, and the unutterable sorrows; and there was the ever impelling
question, How can humanity justify or God forgive? Human hate demands no such toll;
ambition and greed must be denied it. If misunderstanding must take blame, then let us
banish it.*
    —Dedication at the Tomb of the Unknown Soldier, November 12,
1921

Harding appointed Charles Evans Hughes as Secretary of State, Herbert
Hoover as Secretary of Commerce (unfortunately for Harding and the government, Hoover turned him down as Secretary of Interior). Andrew Mellon became Secretary of Treasury, and Charles Dawes (born in Marietta, Ohio), was
appointed to head the newly formed Bureau of the Budget, which consolidated
the disorganized, congressionally-dominated Federal budget. General Leonard
Wood was appointed governor-general of the Philippines. To solve the depression in farm prices after the boom times of 1914-1919, Harding appointed
Henry C. Wallace, an Iowa farmer, writer and editor (and father of one of Franklin
Roosevelt's vice presidents). Taft finally attained his life long dream of appointment as Chief Justice of the Supreme Court. It should also be noted that Florence Kling Harding had been a strong proponent of women's right to vote.

Most of Harding's other appointments were undistinguished. Three were

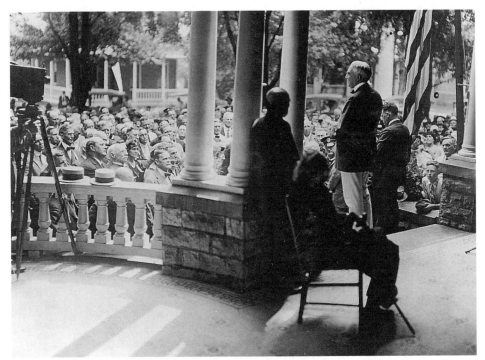

Even well into the twentieth century, Ohioans still campaigned on their porches.

terrible: Charles Forbes as head of war risk insurance, Thomas Miller as alien property custodian, and Senator Albert Fall as Secretary of Interior. One was questionable, Harry Daugherty as Attorney General.

The first major initiative of Harding and Hughes was to call an arms conference to halt the escalating arms race, especially in Navy ships. This resulted ultimately in a treaty limiting the types and gross tonnage for naval ships of the United States, Great Britain, Japan, France, and Italy. The treaty may have hampered the Japanese, who were already coveting China and other parts of Asia.

As a question of good will, and without admitting error, the United States offered Colombia $20 million, essentially for the takeover of Panama during the Theodore Roosevelt administration.

Against the advice of many, including the Duchess, Harry Daugherty, and the American Legion, he pardoned Eugene V. Debs, labor leader and Socialist candidate for President, and 23 others who had been convicted under wartime sedition acts by the Wilson administration. Typically, Harding who liked to deal with people directly met with Debs during the Christmas season of 1921 just before his release, and like Norman Thomas, Debs found Harding likable and decent.

Harding was a personal friend of Elbert Gary, head of U. S. Steel, the then-dominant steel company. The normal work week for steel workers in 1921 was twelve hours a day, seven days a week. With unusual persistence Harding suggested to Gary and other steel leaders an eight hour day for six days a week. The executives said that the change would destroy their industry but after Harding's death in 1923 the industry changed to what he had proposed.

Harding's Civil Rights record was a notable improvement on Wilson's. Taft had appointed many blacks to important sub-cabinet jobs. Wilson, born in the South, removed them. Harding reinstated the Taft policy. He also made a transcendent speech in Birmingham, Alabama, on October 21, 1921, that still rings true. He told a mixed and segregated audience that democracy in the United States. was a lie, "until the Negro was granted political and economic equality"; and that "political, economic and educational equality would not only help American democracy, but the South itself."

B. The Scandals

My God this is a hell of a job! I have no trouble with my enemies. I can take care of my enemies all right. But my damn friends, my God-damn friends...they're the ones that keep me walking the floor nights!
—To William Allen White in June 1923 prior to Harding's "Voyage of Understanding" to the West Coast and Alaska

1. Veterans' Bureau

Among the worst Harding appointees was Charles Forbes. Forbes had been appointed by Wilson as director of the Pearl Harbor Naval base construction. He was charming and bright but had a checkered past. He had joined the Army and deserted, suffering no ill consequences. In World War I, as a signal corps officer, he was so brave and effective under fire that he was awarded the Congressional Medal of Honor and made a lieutenant colonel. After World War I, the care of veterans was disorganized and haphazard. Harding reorganized it and put all the agencies involved into a new Veterans Bureau with Forbes in charge.

Forbes bilked the government in two ways. He got control of supplies at Perry Point, Maryland, and working with favored contractors, bought supplies at exorbitant prices, selling "surpluses" at a fraction of their value. At least once, new supplies coming in the front door would be declared surplus and shipped to a favored contractor out the back door without even being stored. He also sold drugs, often in short supply at hospitals, on the black market. The other scheme was to build veterans' hospitals all at inflated prices and pocket the difference.

Forbes's inevitable downfall was caused by two things. Neither Harry Daugherty nor Dr. Charles Sawyer, Harding personal physician from Marion, trusted Forbes. Forbes also liked the ladies. He made the mistake of having an affair with the wife of one of his "business" partners.

Sawyer, another Harding appointee, suspected fraud at Perry Point and told Harding. Harding was offended but sent two Army officers to check. For whatever reason, they told a relieved Harding that they found nothing. But Sawyer persisted, taking the U. S. Surgeon General to Perry Point. The fraud was confirmed.

The last scene we have of Harding, the people person, with Forbes is Harding in an upstairs room of the White House holding Forbes by the shirt saying, "You yellow rat! You double crossing bastard! If you ever..." At that point they were interrupted by an inadvertent visitor. Forbes and his general counsel, Charles Cramer, resigned and Cramer committed suicide. Forbes served two years in Federal prison.

2. Teapot Dome

Senator Albert Fall was one of the few senators who had been in a gun battle. Born in Frankfort, Kentucky, he went west at a young age to find his fortune. He became a miner, rancher, and lawyer in New Mexico and learned to speak Spanish fluently. He knew much about Mexican culture and law and impressed Harding with his skills at poker.

Historically because the United States has so much land in the West, the Secretary of the Interior is a westerner. When Herbert Hoover, from Iowa and California, turned down interior for commerce, Harding selected Fall. The choice was popular in the Senate, and he was unanimously approved without hearings.

The land between the Pacific coast states and the great plains is often a mystery to many Americans (which should argue for moving the capital to Kansas City, or at least St. Louis). There are two groups that are very fervent about the West: (1) exploiters, who see the west as a raw resource, with mountains to be mined, water to be dammed, forests to be slashed, wild animals to be killed, all for private profit in the name of "economic development"; and (2) the conservationists who look at the beauty of the West with almost religious awe. Fall was clearly of the school of exploitation. He thought that the land of the West should be privately held and that there should be no Department of Interior. People like John Muir were clearly on the other side.

The history of these contending forces goes back a long way. Yellowstone was established during the Grant administration; Yosemite became a national park during the administration of Benjamin Harrison. Theodore Roosevelt who had lived on a ranch in the West had a mixed record. He streched the Antiquities Act to set aside Grand Canyon, Olympic Mountain, and other sites as national monuments. On the other hand his appointees Gifford Pinchot and James R. Garfield emphasized management of Federal lands. Garfield authorized the Hetch Hetchy dam that ultimately caused a large portion of Yosemite to be split out of the park. Taft, who considered himself a conservationist tried to steer a middle course. His first Secretary of Interior, Richard Ballinger, got in an unwinnable fight with Pinchot, and this was one of the reasons that caused Roosevelt to challenge Taft in 1912.

By the appointment of Fall, Harding seemed to side with the exploiters. Early in his administration, Edwin Denby, a Marine veteran and not very competent secretary of the Navy, who knew little about the West and its oil resources, asked Fall if he would manage the Navy's oil reserves. Fall agreed and Harding signed an executive order transferring control to the interior department. The most important of these reserves were at Elk Hills, California, and Teapot Dome, Wyoming.

There were several problems with the reserves. Title to the land was not always clear. Some companies thought they had the right to drill on the reservations. Oil in underground reservoirs could also be drained by wells located adjacent to the reservoirs (offset drilling).

During the Wilson administration, bids were requested from offset drillers, giving the U. S. Government a portion of the oil drilled. The bid most favorable to the government at Elk Hills was submitted by Edward Doheny, a Democrat, who had worked at mining with Fall when they were both young men. Doheny subsequently hired William McAdoo, Wilson's son-in-law and potential Democratic 1920 Presidential candidate, and Franklin Lane, Wilson's former interior secretary. Lane, of the exploitation school, had been accused of awarding dubious claims to drillers at Elk Hills.

Under the law passed during the Wilson administration, Federal profits from offset drilling would go to the general Treasury, except for $500,000 per year, which would go to the Navy. Some in the Navy thought they were losing their reserves and getting a small fraction of the actual value. The Navy was already worried about the Japanese threat in the Pacific. It wanted oil and oil storage tanks at various ports but especially in the Pacific, at Pearl Harbor in Hawaii. Fall hit upon the idea of bartering the U. S. share of oil for certificates good for oil, oil storage facilities, and other Navy needs.

In April of 1922, Fall leased the Teapot Dome reserve to Harry Sinclair's newly created Mammoth Oil Company (Sinclair had Teddy Roosevelt's son, Archie, on his staff). He also gave Doheny first option on future leases for Elk Hills in exchange for certificates for loading docks and storage facilities at Pearl Harbor. In view of the Japanese attack in World War II, this seemed like a very prescient decision.

There were, however, several problems. At Teapot Dome, only Sinclair was given the opportunity to bid. Fall kept the award secret. Finally, Sinclair and other oil company presidents set up the Continental Trading Company in Canada, which purchased Teapot Dome oil from Mammoth at one price and on the same day sold it to the oil companies at an increased price. Thus the company officers were stealing from their own companies. Most damaging to Fall, however, was that Doheny had given Fall $100,000. Sinclair had given Fall more than $300,000 worth of certificates. Fall, whose ranch was deeply in debt, claimed the Doheny money was a loan and that Sinclair had bought a one-third share of his ranch.

Teapot Dome involved many complications and a large cast of characters, including Ned McLean, co-owner of the Hope diamond; two of the Roosevelt sons; Gifford Pinchot; and Senator Thomas J. Walsh of Montana. In 1931 Fall was convicted of taking a bribe from Doheny. Doheny was found not guilty of giving the bribe. Sinclair was convicted of contempt of the Senate and tampering with a jury. The association with Doheny effectively finished the political career of William McAdoo, a leading Democratic candidate for President. Col. Robert Stewart was fired from his job as president of Standard Oil of Indiana for his role in Continental Trading Company.

3. Around Daugherty

No charge against me was ever proven in court.
—Harry M. Daugherty

Harry Daugherty was a fixer-lobbyist of a type common to both parties. They know how to get things done at the edge of the law, things that may be legal but not necessarily ethical. It is to their own interest to often exaggerate their influence and Daugherty certainly did. Daugherty's initial venue was Columbus. He met Harding there but was not particularly close to him until 1918 or so when Daugherty conceived and executed the plan that ultimately made Harding President. Harding was grateful and, despite warnings, made Daugherty attorney general.

Daugherty considered himself a realist. He knew the world and he knew Harding. He thought of himself as the gentle Harding's protector. One of the early scandals involved Thomas Miller, a well-to-do Congressman from Delaware. Miller had enlisted in the Army during World War I and, while serving in France, rose from a private to lieutenant colonel. After the war he was one of the co-founders of the American Legion and became director of the Republican National Campaign Committee. Harding appointed him custodian of alien property. There was a lot of property seized from the Germans when the United States entered the war against them. At the end of the war, the custodian was to oversee the assets from this property. Miller was involved with a property of American Metal Company. Working with another lawyer-fixer, John T. King of New York, Miller arranged to "return" $7 million to one Thomas Merton, a former German military officer who claimed the property had been sold by oral contract to an organization in Switzerland prior to U.S. involvement in the war. Merton was given checks and cash equivalents for the $7 million. Generous payments were made to Miller, King, and others. Miller and King were both indicted. King died before the trial, but Miller was convicted of bribery and served thirteen months in prison.

The largest scandal close to Daugherty was that of Jesse Smith. Smith was a Washington Court House department store owner, gossip, and dandy who became a close friend of Daugherty. When Daugherty became Attorney General, Smith went off to Washington with him. They lived together (Daugherty's wife was an invalid who stayed in Ohio), and Smith had an unofficial office near Daugherty's in the Justice Department. There was lots of crime in 1920, much of it involving prohibition. The word got around that if something needed to be fixed, Jesse was the man to see. There were literally dozens of charges of illegal or improper influence against Smith. He and Daugherty both had suspicious accounts in Daugherty's brother's bank in Washington Court House. When Harding got word of some of Smith's activities, he cut off further contact with him. Smith, whose ego was fragile, committed suicide. Harry Daugherty, the realist, burned records of the Smith and Daugherty accounts. Daugherty was indicted with Miller and tried twice but never convicted of anything.

Harding: *If you knew of a great scandal in our administration, would you for the good of the country and the party expose it publicly or would you bury it?*

Herbert Hoover: *Publish it and at least get credit for integrity on your side.*
—Conversation in June 1923

Some day, the people will understand what some of my erstwhile friends have done to me in these critical times when I depended so much upon them.
—Conversation with Joe Mitchell Chapple, November 1922

C. Voyage of Understanding; and Death

In 1923 the scandals began to come to Harding's attention. It threatened his place in history. His never robust health was deteriorating. He had an enlarged heart, high blood pressure, and probably arteriosclerosis. As always, he was restless; the White House was like a cage. He wanted to get out and see the people. He decided to make a long rail and steamship trip to the West and Alaska. Before going, the not very religious but always intuitive Harding said he felt a "conscious spiritual influence" over his action.

This was the context of his final trip. He would crusade for the United States to join the World Court. It was a very strenuous trip, bizarrely paralleling Wilson's near fatal trip of five years before. His first major stop would be St. Louis, in the heart of "isolationist" country, just as previously he had gone to Alabama to plead for Negro rights. Like other Republican leaders such as Benjamin Harrison, William McKinley, and William Howard Taft, he thought the idea of an international body resolving disputes could help prevent wars. It was different from Wilson's League with all its encumbrances. When he got to Denver he spoke to soldiers wounded in the war. He promised that next time in war, "money would be conscripted as well as people." He went to Zion National Park and to Yellowstone and then took a sea voyage to Alaska.

I want America to have something of a spiritual ideal. I am seeking American sentiment in favor international justice. I want America to play her part in helping to abolish war.
—Speech in Salt Lake City, Voyage of Understanding, June 1923

Perhaps the "conscious spiritual influence" was speaking to him, or perhaps like John Muir and others he was inspired by the awesome beauty of the West;

perhaps he wanted to offset Fall and Lane and the other exploiters. At Jackson Hole, in the sight of the Grand Tetons, he condemned the thought that the West "should fall into the hands of bonanza corporations seeking to exploit it for profit of stockholders." At Vancouver, British Columbia, where he became the first American President to speak in Canada, he made a homey reference to neighborliness. After he saw Alaska, in a speech written for him by Herbert Hoover, he said he would not see Alaska turned over to exploiters " to loot as the possibility of profit arises...life in lovely, wonderful Alaska must (be treated) as an end, not a means." In mid-speech Harding faltered, grabbed the podium, and dropped the speech. Hoover picked it up and re-sorted it while Harding finished.

That night Harding complained of indigestion. Dr. Sawyer blamed it on bad crabmeat. Some thought he might have had a heart attack. Other speeches were canceled and he traveled to San Francisco where he was confined to bed for five days. On the evening of August 23, 1923, Duchess was reading him an article from *The Saturday Evening Post, "A Calm View of a Calm Man."* His last words were, "That's good, read some more." He probably died of a stroke.

~

V. Burial and Dedication of Tomb

Harding's death was a shock to the country who at that time knew nothing about Teapot Dome. An amount of $700,000 was raised from around the country for a Roman style tomb in Marion. By the time it was completed President Calvin "Silent Cal" Coolidge would not dedicate it. The next President, Herbert Hoover, was also hesitant but finally on June 16, 1931, he dedicated it.

His was the mind and character fitted for a task where the one transcendent need was the healing quality of gentleness and friendliness....Here was a man whose soul was seared by a great disillusionment. We saw him gradually weaken, not only from physical exhaustion, but also mental anxiety. Warren Harding had a dim realization that he had been betrayed by a few of the men whom he believed were his devoted friends. That was the tragedy of the life of Warren Harding.

—President Herbert Hoover at the dedication of Harding's tomb, June 16, 1931

● Visiting Harding Sites

The Roman-style tomb is at Delaware Avenue at Vernon Heights Boulevard, Marion. It is impressive. The President Harding Home and Museum is at 380 Mount Vernon Avenue, Ohio Route 95. There is a Marion County museum with exhibits about Harding at 169 East Church Street, one block east of Main. *The Marion Star* remains the daily newspaper of Marion although in a different facility from Harding's day. Another interesting point about Marion is that it is the site of a natural spring, which caused William Henry Harrison and his troops to stop and camp there during the war of 1812 on his way to Upper Sandusky.

● Works Relevant to Understanding the Warren G. Hardings

A. Biographical

Adams, Samuel Hopkins. 1939. *Incredible Era: The Life and Times of Warren Gamaliel Harding.* Boston: Houghton Mifflin Company.

Adams was a journalist who didn't have access to the Harding papers. He summarizes the conventional view of Harding in the late 1920s and 1930s. He also wrote *Revelry,* a thinly disguised novel based on the Harding administration.

Russell, Francis. 1968. *The Shadow of Blooming Grove: Warren G. Harding in His Times.* New York: McGraw-Hill Book Company.

This is a first class biography, fair and comprehensive. It tells the story of Ohio politics from the 1880s to the 1920s and how Harding fit in. It also describes many of the characters that Harding encountered. In the first edition copy which I read, there are several minor errors and also exclusions that were to include passages for the letters between Harding and Carrie Phillips, sealed under court order by an Ohio judge.

Sinclair, Andrew. 1965. *The Available Man: The Life Behind the Masks of Warren Gamaliel Harding.* New York: The Macmillan Company.

This is an intriguing book by a British professor. He states the importance of myth and how Harding used myth to propel himself into the Presidency. The theses of the book seem credible, although one can still wonder if the League of Nations could have solved anything and what reasonable economic and agriculture policies would have been for the early 1920s. I think Sinclair, who did have access to the Harding papers, accurately characterizes the roles of both Hardings and Daugherty.

B. Non-biographical

●**Allen, Frederick Lewis.** 1931. *Only Yesterday.* New York: Bantam Books.
The title is a little dated now. This is a book about the Roaring Twenties, a remarkable decade of profound change, in many ways comparable to the 1960s. The book is journalistic in style, easy to read.

●**Anderson, Sherwood.** 1919. *Winesburg, Ohio.* New York: A Penguin Book.
Anderson was born in Camden, Ohio, and ran a paint factory in Elyria, Ohio. If Harding appealed to a nostalgia for small town and rural Midwest, Anderson and Sinclair Lewis presented the other side. Anderson, whose book is a series of related stories, quarreled with the unnatural restraints of the small town's society.

●**Britton, Nan.** 1927. *The President's Daughter.* New York: Elizabeth Ann Guild.
This is the famous book that is probably generally truthful about the relationship between the author and Harding. It is interesting and revealing, but the language is a little overwrought.

●**Cox, James M.** 1946. *Journey Through My Years.* New York: Simon and Schuster.
Cox was the unsuccessful Democratic candidate for President in 1920. He led an eventful life from his birth near Jacksonburg, Ohio, to his ownership of major papers in Dayton, Miami, and Atlanta (which today make up the core of Cox Communications, a major media company); his reform governorship of Ohio when the workmen's compensation act was first implemented; and his friendships, especially with the Wright brothers, their sister, and Franklin D. Roosevelt. The book rambles a bit but is interesting. There is every indication that Cox would have been a better President than Harding, but Cox supported the ideals of Wilson and the League of Nations when the country was tired of both.

●**Lewis, Sinclair.** 1920. *Main Street.* Widely available in paperback.
Lewis was from a small town in Minnesota. The book, attacking smugness and complacency, does not idealize its small town, Gopher Prairie, Minnesota.

●**Lynd, Robert S. and Helen Merrell.** 1929 *Middletown.* New York: Harcourt Brace World.

This is a classic of social anthropology, a detailed study of Muncie, Indiana, in the period from 1890 to 1925. Andrew Sinclair points out that there are many similarities between Muncie and Harding's Marion, Ohio, during this period. The Lynds did a follow-up study in 1937. Many others have followed that.

●**McLean, Evalyn Walsh and C. Boyden Sparkes.** 1936. *Father Struck It Rich.* Boston: Little Brown and Co.

This is the story of the miner's daughter who married the publisher of *The Washington Post and Cincinnati Enquirer,* bought the Hope diamond, and was friends with the "Duchess."

●**Noggle, Burl.** 1965. *Teapot Dome, Oil and Politics in the 1920's.* New York: Norton and Co.

This book widens the context of the scandal, pointing out that both political parties were involved with oil, and there was a continuing battle between conservationists and exploiters. This is an interesting book with lots of fascinating details.

●**Smith, Gene.** 1964. *When the Cheering Stopped.* New York: Morrow and Co.

This is the tragic story of Woodrow Wilson's collapse on his Western trip, and last eighteen months in office. Wilson's situation was partly responsible for the 25th Amendment to the Constitution providing for replacement of an incapacitated President.

●**Sophocles.** *Antigone* (estimated to be written about 440 B. C.) Widely available in paperback.

This is a great play by one of the world's greatest playwrights. It is about a tyrant's refusal to properly bury a soldier and the tragedy that ensues.

●**Tarkington, Booth.** 1921. *Alice Adams.* Garden City, NY: Doubleday, Page and Co.

Tarkington, a versatile writer from Indiana, also wrote about small town life in the Midwest. He is more gentle than either Sherwood Anderson or Sinclair Lewis. This book is about the struggle of a marginal family in a small town-like environment.

Afterwords

If on this continent we merely build another country of great but unjustly divided material prosperity we shall have done nothing.

—Theodore Roosevelt

The Civil War may have been built into the Constitution and the institution of slavery. It was built on freedom, but sanctioned slavery. Our two most eloquent Presidents warned us. Jefferson worried about "a firebell in the night," when the morality of slavery was discussed in the context of accepting Missouri as a slave state. Lincoln, of course, believed that no nation could endure permanently "half slave and half free." Looking backwards, it is obvious that slavery had to be abolished. The tragedy was that it had to be abolished in such a cataclysmic way.

Relating the volatile national condition to our first Ohio President, William Henry Harrison, Harrison wasn't a joke who made a long speech standing in the rain, catching pneumonia and dying. He was an intelligent, hospitable, and patriotic man, who was tough enough to lead western troops, and smart enough to govern the North West territories. By temperament he was a conciliator. If ever the country needed conciliation it was in the 1840s and 1850s. Harrison's untimely death deprived us of that opportunity.

U. S. Grant always had a bad image—that of a scruffy alcoholic. Grant, an exceptional learner, was a quiet, modest man. Unlike most politicians and many military men he never promoted himself. Some think he was the greatest general in the Civil War. He stands beside Lincoln in victory. By temperament he was not suited to politics (or business). He was too straight-forward and honest, not Machiavellian enough. The post Civil War period, when Grant was President, was one of the most difficult in our entire history. Grant, too, would have been a conciliator. There were too many forces working against conciliation. Grant, like the proud but ineffectual Andrew Johnson, was caught in the middle.

There were many scandals after the Civil War, just as there were after World War I and World War II, our largest wars. Grant was partly to blame and partly unlucky. His most trustworthy staff officer, John Rawlins, died of tuberculosis soon after Grant became President. Grant's most untrustworthy of staff officers, Orville Babcock, betrayed him. Grant, the organizer of victory in the Civil War, was not ruthless enough to get rid of him. Sixteen years after he left the presidency, Grant, the cigar chomper, developed a tragic kind of cancer of the soft palate and esophagus. He had been swindled out of his money. He was broke and sick. Through great pain in writing his *Memoirs* he transcended everything, his transcendence a model to us all.

Rutherford Birchard Hayes is often used as a metaphor for obscurity. The 1876 election was questionable. But for some reason the intimidation in the South of pro-Hayes black voters seems to be ignored. Hayes, like Lincoln, came to the Presidency as a former Whig. The Whigs believed in a limited Presidency. Hayes, a well-educated, decent, honest, intelligent and humane man with a vivacious and dedicated wife, served the country in a selfless way. He stood beside Lincoln in his advocacy of human rights for poor and minorities. I personally think we should honor Hayes. Any time we get a President that good we should feel lucky.

James A. Garfield was a man of great intellect and great energy who had a checkered career. In current business terms, he "thought outside the box." Some thought he was Machiavellian. Undoubtedly he had a touch of that. In the Civil War he helped get rid of a friend, William Rosecrans, who seemed to be an ineffective general. As President he got two malefactors out of the Senate, Conkling and Platt. Garfield might have had the right mixture of intellect, energy, and Machiavellianism to have become a great President. Sadly, we will never know.

The other Harrison, Benjamin, was in many ways a model President. He was an intelligent, resourceful, workaholic lawyer. He treated the nation as a client. He was not lovable. He could be cold, blunt, and austere. On slavery he didn't *think* it was wrong, he *knew* it was wrong. In the Civil War he fought with great zeal against it. As President he was an early advocate of national parks, reform of the military, and arbitration to settle international disputes. His career deserves more attention than it gets. One of the central lessons of Benjamin Harrison's life is that unlikeable people can become good Presidents.

William McKinley seems old-fashioned and perhaps a little pompous today. Even in his own day he was regarded as a popular politician with his ear to the ground. But McKinley offers lots of lessons. We should remember the courage of a nineteen-year-old at Antietam and four years of front-line battle. We should remember him for his noble patience with his wife, whose illness was a fitting symbol of tragedy in life. Most of all we should remember how he delayed and blocked the war with Spain until Congress almost passed a bill for war without his support. Like many front-line soldiers, he never talked about his service in the war, or heroism. I think he remembered and did all he could to prevent others from experiencing what he had. I call that nobility of character.

William Howard Taft, our good-natured 350-pound President, operated in the shadow of Theodore Roosevelt, a President with the greatest natural sense of public relations. Taft, an infectiously cheerful man, was unhappy as President. That should not blind us to achievements, however. Taft was a sincere conservationist. Glacier National Park came into existence during his administration and his second interior secretary relentlessly promoted the idea of a national park service. This was important since two other Federal agencies, the Forest Service and the Bureau of Reclamation, were strongly committed to economic development. As a lawyer he had serious reservations about Theodore Roosevelt's setting aside Federal land for conservation by executive order, rather than law. He had a point. His administration initiated more than twice as many anti-trust cases than Theodore Roosevelt's. Finally he tackled the tariff, something Theodore Roosevelt would not do. Although Taft generally failed in his goal of tariff reform, should we condemn those who try and miss more than those who never try? What Taft lacked was flair, a sense of public relations. To his lawyerly mind and cautious soul, government public relations smacked of dishonesty. Taft, like Hayes, did what he thought was right without careful political calculation. That used to be called character. (Harry Truman, a partisan Democrat who ran a scandal-plagued administration, also had that quality, which is one of the reasons he is admired).

Finally we come to Harding. I must admit I dreaded reading about him. Harding was not unintelligent, a man who took a minor weekly and turned it into the major paper in a growing and prosperous town. He also proved to be a model employer who gave his employees stock in the company, something worthy of emulation even today. Politically he plotted a strategy that carried him to the state senate, the lieutenant governership, and the U. S. Senate. Like both Harrisons, Hayes, and Garfield, he was an accidental President. When he got there he was probably fatally ill. He had Teapot Dome and other scandals. He, too, was betrayed by friends. Harding's finest hour was probably in Birmingham, Alabama, when before a mass audience he pleaded for equal rights for Negroes.

Several Ohio Presidents may have been wrong about tariffs (exceptions Grant, Garfield, and Taft). This was special interest legislation at its worst. The entire country paid a tax that generally benefited the few. On the major issue of the nineteenth century about the value of money, I probably would not have been sympathetic to them at the time but now must admit that they were probably right. The industrialization of America was often brutal and chaotic. Presidents like Hayes, Benjamin Harrison, McKinley, Taft, and even Harding tried to humanize the process. Perhaps they could have done more.

Of course the greatest issue in our country is human equality and civil rights. It is what still makes us "last best hope on earth." It is expressed succinctly in our national creed: "All men are created equal." * The good thing about the Ohio Presidents is that they were *all* on the right side of the issue. Five of them fought directly against slavery. All sought to aid oppressed people, including ex-slaves or their descendants, later becoming identified with issues called civil rights. Grant and Hayes felt special empathy for the poor or oppressed everywhere. This is a worthy legacy, one of which we should all be proud. It is a legacy which we still need to build upon.

If you remember anything about the Ohio Presidents, let it be their commitment and their actions to carry out the nation's creed: *All men are created equal.*

—James Burris Cash

* *The term "men" was used rhetorically. It, of course, includes all people. Its greatness as a creed is that it is as valid today as it was in 1776. Jefferson, the intuitive revolutionary, knew what he was doing.*

Appendix

Some Comments on Evaluating U. S. Presidents

Periodically one sees lists of Presidential rankings by historians. That serious historians would condense their judgment in such a simplistic way surprises me for they, above all, should understand how complex the interaction of man and times can be. Having said that, one may still look at the rankings and comment. My own view is that the historians are correct in the Presidents generally rated at the top: Abraham Lincoln and George Washington. Below them, however, I have many questions.

For the period 1812-1923 to some extent covered by this book, I would cite several examples. The first would be James Madison, a legitimate hero in this country. He was a longtime associate of the writer of our national creed, Thomas Jefferson, and he participated in writing the Constitution and The Federalist papers. Yet it was his administration that bungled the War of 1812. My own conclusion is that there was no American war handled more poorly, including the Vietnamese War. There was also a serious economic downturn during the Madison administration, and if Presidents are blamed for economic downturns (a dubious proposition) Madison can be blamed for that also. It was the worst of all worlds: non-prosperity and war.

In Presidential rankings serious economic difficulties seem to count against some Presidents but not others. Two Presidents are blamed for panics or depressions: Martin Van Buren and Herbert Hoover. Why? I think it had a lot to do with their personalities. Van Buren was a clever backroom operator who probably deserves credit for some of Andrew Jackson's success, but he wasn't *likable*. Hoover, a bright, idealistic, mining engineer, had no charisma or sense of public relations.

There was a panic in 1873, but Grant is usually not blamed for it. There were panics or depressions in 1884 and 1893 without scapegoat Presidents. There were sharp panics in 1907 under Theodore Roosevelt, in 1920 under the seriously ailing Woodrow Wilson, and a serious decline or second depression in 1938 under the hero of the Great Depression, Franklin D. Roosevelt. Yet none of these Presidents are ever blamed. Of course, all of these Presidents are admirable in certain ways especially Franklin D. Roosevelt, a crippled man with an unquenchable spirit and a remarkable wife. He was very resourceful and energetic in trying to deal with the Great Depression, but it is questionable that he cured it. What seemed to cure the Great Depression was the mobilization for World War II when Roosevelt undoubtedly became a great wartime leader. The main point is that if economic downturns are blamed on Presidents, then all should be blamed.

Let us consider the worst Presidents. Often Grant, Harding, and Nixon are at the bottom, which is questionable. The key issue is: Did scandals associated with these Presidents have the greatest long term negative consequences for the country? The answer is, of course not. By magnitudes the worst tragedy this country ever faced was the Civil War. From 1841 to 1861 there were seven Presidents. Most of them did nothing to halt our slide toward war, and some of them exacerbated it. Two of the seven, the southern-born William Henry Harrison and Zachary Taylor, might have done something. They were both strong nationalists with practical intelligence and talented cabinet officers. It was perhaps tragic that they both died before having great impact as Presidents, Harrison after one month in office, Taylor after one year and four months in office. James K. Polk served from 1847 to 1851, a period that gave us the Mexican War, criticized by such diverse people as U. S. Grant and Henry David Thoreau. Some of Polk's actions in pursuing that war are questionable, and although he was a dedicated nationalist and a hard-working President, his legacy remains unclear. That leaves four candidates for the worst, and I suggest historians pick from the following: John Tyler, Millard Fillmore, Franklin Pierce, and James Buchanan.

What about the Ohioans? I think six of them were blamed for being soldiers, Grant, like Eisenhower, a West Point graduate, especially so. Historians are conscious of the European tradition where soldiers like Julius Caesar and Napoleon often dominate their governments. They did not want that in America, and they have a point. Of course Grant, like Zachary Taylor, was a very un-military military man. That some historians fail to give him full credit for his achievements in the Civil War leads one to wonder about a more general bias against Grant. As President he did have his scandals, but his scandals should be compared to those of Truman, a President generally admired by historians. Hayes, Garfield, Benjamin Harrison, and McKinley were not professional military men but citizen-soldiers. It should be recognized that the cause they fought for was just. In the Civil War the two sides were not morally equivalent. Although the Confederacy had a point about states' rights and the tariff, the main issues of the war were the indivisibility of the Union and a choice between two economic systems, one based on slavery and one opposed to slavery. Although many Confederates fought with courage, tenacity, and even humanity, their fundamental cause was not a good one. If the Union had been divided the United States would probably have become like Europe with almost continuous warfare. Slavery was a repugnant institution. With the five Ohio Civil War veterans, we should first of all honor them for risking their lives in a just cause.

Three "great" or "near-great" Presidents should be carefully evaluated: Andrew Jackson, Theodore Roosevelt, and Woodrow Wilson. Jackson was a hero to my mother's family, early settlers in Indiana who thought Jackson opened the government to ordinary people like them. Jackson was very forceful and somewhat arbitrary. By implementing his "spoils system" he may have deprofessionalized government from the 1830s on. The struggle for civil service in the nineteenth century and our complex and wasteful system of government today may be Jackson legacies. One of Jackson's major policies was to fight and eventually destroy the National Bank. This is a hard issue to understand, today except for the condescending arrogance of the bank leadership. Jackson's victory over the bank seemed like one for the common people. But isn't it most likely that this, and the subsequent Jackson economic policies caused the Panic of 1837 that Van Buren was blamed for? In our relationships with American Indians, Jackson was probably our most active and aggressive President in removing American Indians to the West. Undoubtably his policies reflected main-stream thinking of the time and yet one cannot help contrasting this with the regrets expressed by Rutherford B. Hayes about the treatment of Indians.

Finally, Jackson is appropriately credited with challenging South Carolina and its theory on the nullification of laws it did not like. Jackson again looks like a hero, appearing much more far-seeing than the redoubtable John C. Calhoun, but in less than thirty years South Carolina led the rebellion in the South by voting unanimously for secession. Was this inevitable or could a less bellicose, more mediative President have changed the course of history?

A comparison of Theodore Roosevelt's record with Taft's is instructive. Taft instigated more anti-trust cases, and their fundamental difference on conservation was that Roosevelt thought setting land aside land by executive order was adequate, while Taft thought it should be done by law. Taft was probably right since any executive order can be nullified by another executive order. Teddy was a conservation hero for setting aside the Grand Canyon and Mount Olympus, yet his administration also authorized a dam in what was part of Yosemite, ultimately causing the park to be split.

Taft tried to reform the tariff, a task that Teddy would not try. Teddy gave the people of Latin America a reason to hate the United States by dramatically aiding the splitting-off of the province of Panama from Colombia. Could not quiet diplomacy have worked with fewer negative long-term consequences? Teddy thought that nations proved themselves through war. It is hard to forgive him for saying that McKinley had the backbone of a chocolate eclair for not leaping into the Spanish-American War. McKinley was a front-line soldier for four years. One battle that McKinley participated in, Antietam, saw more American casualties *in one hour* than the entire Spanish-American War. Teddy would have been most dangerous had he been elected in 1912. When World War I began in 1914 he chided Woodrow Wilson for not getting the United States involved. Wilson probably saved hundreds of thousands of Americans from that merciless slaughter by not listening to Roosevelt. Ironically, if Teddy had not challenged Taft in 1912 but waited to reseek the Presidency until 1916, he with his special brand of force and charisma might have succeeded in forcing a peace on Europe more effectively than Wilson.

Roosevelt had great energy, he was a talented writer and phrase maker with a lively and attractive family, and a man of courage and conviction who fought for good causes like conservation and anti-trust. On the other hand, he was a shameless self-dramatist and probably the President with the most natural sense of public relations. One of Roosevelt's longest lasting legacies may be the widespread use of governmental public relations, *i. e.,* disciplined deception.

Woodrow Wilson, also a man of great energy, was an intellectual, a prolific writer, a university professor, and a reformest college president. As President he initially kept the country out of World War I, then led it into the war, and finally through the Treaty of Versailles and League of Nations tried to lead the world to lasting peace. Ultimately he failed and it cost him his health if not his life.

The Wilson administration had other problems. If one looks at the entire

Teapot Dome as a generic term for oil leasing, the scandal was not strictly a Harding and Republican scandal. The leasing of Federal oil lands began under the Wilson administration, and like many financial-business scandals, involved *both* political parties. William McAdoo, Wilson's Secretary of the Treasury and son-in-law, became involved in the oil business as did one of the sons of Theodore Roosevelt. Wilson wasn't personally implicated, but the entire story of Federal oil leasing is much more interesting and instructive than the segment blamed on the Harding administration.

Another un-publicized aspect of the Wilson administration was its racial policies. In general Taft hired blacks for positions in the government, Wilson removed them, and Harding rehired them. To many blacks fighting for equality, Taft and Harding outrank Wilson. Reasons for this are party traditions and constituencies. From the Lincoln administration to that of Franklin D. Roosevelt, the Republican party was generally most sympathetic to blacks and other minorities. The Wilson administration also presided over the notorious Palmer raids involving massive arrests of political and labor agitators, and the jailing of labor leader, Eugene V. Debs, which shows that any political party can be a threat to civil liberties.

Three of our great or near-great Presidents obviously did some very positive things. Jackson was right in proclaiming to ordinary people that the government belongs to them and not some eastern elite. This with Jefferson's immortal words help advance the greatest of ideals in this country. The Carolina-born Jackson was also right in challenging South Carolina's view of the Union. His views of the Union and the practical implications of threats to it by states' defiance were greatly superior to those of Tyler, Pierce, Fillmore, and Buchanan. We owe to Theodore Roosevelt credit for his great energy and resourcefulness for showing what presidential leadership could do and for trying to protect wilderness areas and challenging the sometimes abusive power of big business. Wilson may have tried to achieve the largest objective of all: to bring peace to the world. Thus we credit them. But each of these leaders—like all Presidents—had mixed records.

Thus in my sampling of about 110 years of Presidential tenure, one can find great distortion, double standards, emphasis on some issues and the ignoring of others. Most disconcerting is an overemphasis on personality, rhetoric and public relations, and a failure to consider the long term consequences of actions. True objectivity seems to be lacking. Thus the public seems to be well-served to be skeptical of Presidential rankings.

General Bibliography

A. On the Presidents and the Presidency

Barber, James David. 1972. *The Presidential Character.* Englewood Cliffs, NJ: Prentice Hall, Inc.

This book includes effective often poignant sketches of Presidents from Taft through Nixon. Barber's conclusions are probably outdated, and his method of classifying Presidents seems arbitrary and forced.

Cunliffe, Marcus and the Editors of American Heritage. 1968. *The American Heritage History of the Presidency.* New York: American Heritage Publishing Co., Inc. distributed by Simon and Schuster

This is a well-illustrated and interesting book.

De Gregorio, William A. 1993. *The Complete Guide to U. S. Presidents.* Avenel, NJ: Wings Books, distributed by Random House.

This is a comprehensive and up-to-date book that is a good, quite readable reference book.

Goebel, Dorothy Burne, and Julius Goebel, Jr. 1945. *Generals in the White House.* Garden City, NY: Doubleday, Doran and Company, Inc.

This book includes chapters on W. H. Harrison and Grant and a chapter on Hayes, Garfield, and Benjamin Harrison. Although brief, it is a thorough and logical book of generals and Presidents in the context of their times.

Hess, Stephen. 1966. *American Political Dynasties from Adams to Kennedy.* Garden City, NY: Doubleday & Company, Inc.

This book includes chapters on the Harrisons and the Tafts and other significant political families. It is an interesting book that can lead to speculation about nature vs. nurture (and money). It doesn't give the two Harrison Presidents much credit and is somewhat dated at this point.

Hunt, John Gabriel, (editor). 1995. *The Inaugural Addresses of All the Presidents.* Avenel, NJ: The Library of Freedom, Gramercy Books.

This is a useful and interesting book containing the complete inaugural addresses of all the Presidents.

Lorant, Stephan. 1968. *The Glorious Burden.* New York: Harper & Row.

This is a large, well-illustrated book by the author of biographies of Theodore Roosevelt and Abraham Lincoln.

Schlesinger, Arthur M. Sr. 1949. *Paths to the Present.* The Macmillian Company. Republished 1964. Boston: The Houghton Mifflin Company.

This is a book of miscellaneous essays on American history. The Presidential ratings of Chapter six have become conventional wisdom. Like all conventional wisdom, it should be questioned and tested. (See Appendix.)

B. First Ladies

The importance of the first ladies is often underestimated, especially in the nineteenth century where generally the rigidly constructed roles of the man were public and that of his spouse private. Many of the first ladies were perceptive and intelligent and contributed greatly to their husband's successes. Lucy Webb Hayes, Lucretia Rudolph Garfield, Caroline Scott Harrison, and Helen Herron Taft had superior educations, which they used to benefit their husbands and their country.

Anthony, Carl Sferrazza. 1990. *First Ladies.* 2 Vols., New York: William Morrow and Company, Inc.

This is a two-volume work, the first of which covers the period 1789 to 1961. It is resourcefully written although rather too unsympathetic to Lucy

Hayes, who was warm and gracious as well as being a temperance advocate, a cause now badly out of style; and Caroline Harrison, who not only put up with a grouchy and workaholic husband but tried to bring beauty and art to the White House. Its portraits of the oddly talented and tragic Mary Todd Lincoln and the irrepressible Julia Dent Grant are worth the price of the book.

Klapthor, Margaret Brown. 1994. *The First Ladies.* Washington DC: White House Historical Association with the cooperation of the National Geographic Association.

This is a well-done book of short essays and pictures of all first ladies.

Truman, Margaret. 1995. *First Ladies.* New York: Random House.

Margaret Truman, who grew up with one (underrated) first lady, knew or talked to fifteen others. Her sections on her own mother, the J. Q. Adams family, Mary Todd Lincoln and Lucy Hayes, are excellent. She seems unfair to R. B. Hayes and J. A. Garfield, doesn't cover the dramatic McKinley story, and has minimal coverage of three exceptional women: the well-educated Crete Garfield, the artistic Carrie Harrison, and the intelligent Anna Symmes Harrison.

C. Ohio History and Background

England, J. Merton. (Editor. Published in 1996). *Buckeye Schoolmaster A Chronicle of Midwestern Rural Life 1853-1865.* Bowling Green, OH: Bowling Green Popular Press.

The journals of John M. Roberts, who lived in Madison County, Ohio, from 1833 to 1914, covers much more than school teaching, giving an insight on the times. Roberts, a Democrat, was generally enlightened and intelligent. The exception was his racism. It shows the attitudes of part of the coalition that Hayes, Garfield, and others fought against.

Foster, Emily, (Editor) 1996. *The Ohio Frontier: An Anthology of Early Writings.* Lexington, KY: The University of Kentucky Press.

This book is based upon the letters and diaries of ordinary people settling in the Ohio frontier from 1750 to 1843, a period encompassing parts of the lives of six of Ohio's presidents.

Knepper, George W. 1989. *Ohio and Its People.* Kent, OH: Kent State Press.

This is a comprehensive and readable one-volume history of Ohio. It is generally fair to Ohio's Presidents.

D. Military History and the Civil War

McPherson, James M. 1988. *Battle Cry of Freedom: The Civil War Era.* Oxford, England, New York: Oxford University Press.

This is a modern, objective one-volume history of the Civil War. It is written in a straight-forward style and is astonishingly thorough.

Millett, Allan R. and Maslowski, Peter. 1994. *For the Common Defense, A Military History of the United States.* New York: The Free Press, a Macmillian Company.

This is a biography of the military of the United States and its predecessor colonial governments from 1607 to 1993, showing why our country has had a unique military tradition involving citizen-soldiers. Of the Ohio Presidents, Grant comes across as an effective military leader and administrator. Grant appointee William Tecumseh Sherman made special contributions to the Army by creating professional-military-technical schools, and his protégé, Emory Upton (a New Yorker who had attended Oberlin), re-designed Army tactics and organization based upon *his* experiences in the Civil War. Benjamin Harrison and his Secretary of the Navy, Benjamin F. Tracey, receive credit for starting Navy modernization.

E. On Tariffs

Taussig, F. W. 1931. *Tariff History of the United States.* New York: G. P. Putnam's Sons.

This book is clearly written and objective, explaining in some detail our trade and tariff policies from 1789 to 1930. Most relevant to Ohio's Presidents are the tariffs enacted in 1861 through 1922. The purpose of the 1861 tariff was to raise revenue for the Civil War. Surprisingly the tariff was the main source of Government revenue in the nineteenth century. However, the rationale for most of the tariffs was to protect industry or agriculture. Through the Congressional process—wheeling and dealing and favoritism, if not bribery—the tariff schedules became convoluted, much like the IRS schedules of today for some of the same reasons. Although many Democrats supported high tariffs, this was mainly a Republican issue, one reason why the Republicans became identified as the party of big business. Tariffs often served to raise everybody's prices to help a few. Their positions on tariffs undoubtedly hurt the historical reputations of Benjamin Harrison and William McKinley. Taussig gives credit to the Grant and Garfield administrations for their attempts at tariff reform and to Taft for trying to be constructive and rational in the tariff of 1913.

F. On Money

Timberlake, Richard H. 1933. *Monetary Policy in the United States.* Chicago: The University of Chicago Press.

The volume, availability, and control of money have always been political issues in the United States. The fundamental principles of having dear or cheap money are fairly easy to understand. The technicalities of what makes currencies strong or weak, including use of the gold standard, the printing of greenbacks, monetization of silver and its ratios to gold, and other mechanizations can become very complex. Timberlake, a monetarist, writes about the issues involved from 1789 to the modern Greenspan era of the Federal Reserve.

G. National Parks

Runte, Alfred. 1979. *National Parks: The American Experience.* Lincoln, NE: University of Nebraska Press.

The last seven of Ohio's Presidents were in office during the initial age of building our national parks. (William Henry Harrison came to Ohio when its scenic beauties and ecological richness might have qualified most of the state to become a national park.) This book tells of the long and difficult struggle to establish and maintain national parks. Ohio Presidents and their interior secretaries played key roles in national park development. This book is an excellent one, providing a perspective that I found in no other one.

Credits

(William Henry Harrison) 2, 7, 9, Library of Congress; 11,Cincinnati Historical Society; 12, Rutherford B. Hayes Presidential Center, Fremont, Ohio.

(Grant) 18, Library of Congress (by Mathew Brady); 21, Library of Congress, by Mathew Brady; 22, Orange Frazer Library Collection, taken from dageurreotype made just after graduation; 24, 30, 40, Library of Congress; 38, Orange Frazer Library Collection.

(Hayes) 44, 47, 51, 53, 56, 58, 60, 62, 64, from the Rutherford B. Hayes Presidential Center.

(Garfield) 70, 73, 74, 77, 81, 82, 84, 86, Library of Congress

(Benjamin Harrison) 90, 93, 96 (Kurz & Allison lithograph), 101, 105, Library of Congress

(McKinley) 110, McKinley Museum; 113, Library of Congress; 116, 119, 121, McKinley Museum; 126, 129, Library of Congress; 131, Orange Frazer Library Collection.

(Taft) 136, 137, Orange Frazer Library Collection; 139, Library of Congress; 145, U.S. Army Military History Institute; 148, 150, Library of Congress; 153, Rutherford B. Hayes Presidential Center; 157, the William Howard Taft National Historic site; 158, Library of Congress.

(Harding) 162,164, 168, 173, Library of Congress; 175, Ohio Historical Society

Buttons courtesy collection of Steven Pliskin

Acknowledgments

Many people helped on this book directly and indirectly, and I wish to thank them publicly: my wife, Nancy, who always tolerated with unfailingly good humor my eccentricities, including constant reading and writing, side trips to Civil War battlefields, and frequent non-social if not anti-social behavior. She reviewed and commented on every draft of every chapter. Two of my daughters, Diana C. Lennon and Jennifer C. Konetzny, also reviewed and commented on the book, as did my friends, James M. Gallagher, and Dick and Wilda Skidmore. Dan Strayer, whose grandfather knew Harding, offered positive suggestions.

Lots of institutions were helpful, too: the Hayes Presidential Center, the McKinley Museum and Stark County Historical Society, the Harding home and Grant homes, Lakeview Cemetery in Cleveland, the Montgomery County Library in Dayton and the Wright State Library in Fairborn. Thanks also to the inventors of OHIOLINK, which allows one to request a book from a large number of college libraries throughout Ohio.

Some thanks should go to the authors of the many books documenting the lives and times of the Presidents. Their careful documentation builds a base for essayists like me. I hope that mention in the bibliography gives them appropriate recognition.

Finally this book is about heroes. My own view is that Ohio achieved remarkable things in the period 1840-1920. These achievements seem disproportionate to its size. As we ponder the reasons for that we might give rhetorical thanks to some the people that made it possible—our unsung heroes.

Index

James Burris Cash is currently a business consultant, house-husband, and writer. He has been a steel worker, an oil worker, a truck driver, a teacher, a government contracting officer, and a business executive. He graduated from DePauw University where he majored in liberal arts.
He also attended St. Andrews University in Scotland.
He lives in Kettering, Ohio.